TRUST

CARL WANGMAN AND JUDITH IACUZZI

TRUST

THE HISTORY OF THE ASSOCIATION
FOR CORPORATE GROWTH 1954-2011

Driving Middle Market Growth℠

PUBLISHING™

 www.trafford.com

North America & international
toll-free: 1 888 232 4444 (USA & Canada)
phone: 250 383 6864 ✦ fax: 812 355 4082

CONTENTS

PREFACE

In June 2009, Alan Gelband, an honorary member of the Association for Corporate Growth Global Board of Directors, approached us with the suggestion that we write a history of ACG®. He saw the need to tell the story from the early formation in New York in 1954 to the present.

It would include how chapters began, an appendix of chapter inception dates, and a list of ACG presidents/chairmen and InterGrowth chairs. It would discuss challenging issues as they occurred, such as balancing the needs of a diverse membership, the role of ACG Global® (referred to in earlier days as ACG International to distinguish it from the chapters), and making InterGrowth the centerpiece it is today.

Mr. Gelband suggested that we contact all past presidents of ACG to learn of the challenges that each faced in leading the organization. He also pictured an overview of the history of ACG InterGrowth, including locations, chairs, and highlights of ACG's premier event. He suggested that we explore the financial history of the organization, the role of sponsorship, the governance of the chapters and of ACG Global, and public awareness of ACG as it grew. To finance the research and writing, Mr. Gelband approached Bobby Blumenfeld, executive director of ACG New York. The chapter board agreed with Mr. Blumenfeld's recommendation to fund the writing.

We soon realized that the project would need limits. We regret that we were unable to report about the thousands (yes, thousands) of men and women who have made great contributions to ACG, global and local. We focused on reaching past, present, and upcoming presidents of ACG Global by e-mail, Internet search, and telephone. We wanted to capture their thoughts as leaders then—what were the challenges, what was accomplished. We spoke or corresponded with sixty former and current ACG Global and chapter leaders and created a source document of more than one hundred pages to record their memories and observations. A complete list of all those who contributed is provided in the appendix.

Because the story of ACG is one of the chapters' birth and growth, we also wanted to include histories of some of them. To manage the effort logically, we chose the four chapters that were represented at the first InterGrowth meeting in Mexico City in 1972: New York, Chicago, Toronto, and Los Angeles. We relay their stories in four separate chapters. Because these chapters formed the basis of the global organization, many of their leaders became leaders globally too. Our interviews with these individuals often reflect their dual roles and responsibilities.

It is our hope that in order to make this story more complete, other chapters will follow suit and compile histories of their own.

In the meantime, we thank all the individuals who guided us along the way, conveying their memories in long interviews and follow-up conversations. We thank ACG New York, Mr. Gelband and Mr. Blumenfeld, for conceiving of the idea, asking us to relay it, and for their patience during the eighteen months of its creation. Finally, we thank our staffs and families for their encouragement and support during the research and creative process.

— Carl and Judith

Note:

CHAPTER 1

LAUNCH AND EARLY DEVELOPMENT OF ACG

1954–1968
FORMATION: THE PETER HILTON YEARS

In the early 1950s, a small group of business executives met regularly for lunch in New York City. Theirs was an informal and closed group of senior leaders concerned with how best to grow their companies. Most of them liked the meetings that way, small and familiar.

One member, Peter Hilton, saw it differently. Mr. Hilton had a vision and became the driving force behind a larger, more formalized organization. He suggested the original name, the Association for Corporate Growth and Diversification, Inc., which was incorporated in 1957. It mirrored in part the name of Mr. Hilton's firm, Corporate Diversification, Ltd., of New York.

The official change to the Association for Corporate Growth occurred several years later in 1963, presumably because Mr. Hilton, still active and vibrant, agreed with other leaders—like Murray Sanders of Martin Marietta; Clifford Woods of First National City Bank (Citibank); Tony Hass of General Foods; Neil Bandler and Steve Helpern of Arthur Anderson; John May of William E. Hill; and Carl Hagelin of Marshall & Stevens—that corporate growth was the overarching focus of the organization.

Internal growth was the focus of many meetings in New York. Acquisition as a way to grow is less well documented. But Mr. Hilton was a thought leader who preached about the importance of acquisitions of fully developed products, product lines, and subsidiaries—what he termed "fractional acquisitions"—as the newest and fastest-growing area of corporate growth in the early 1970s.

"These are much easier to effect than a corporate acquisition and can be just as sizable in sales volume and earning potential," said Mr. Hilton at the first InterGrowth speech in 1972. "They rarely involve the government. They rarely involve stockholder approval; they can be acquired for cash or stock or both. They can be acquired with or without real estate; with or without personnel, union obligations, and many of the other encumbrances of the corporate acquisition or even the joint venture… This is one segment of diversification that can no longer be ignored."

1968–1972
OUTREACH AND CHAPTER FORMATION

As the New York group took hold, more attendance came from outside the city, including the cities of Toronto, Chicago, Cleveland, and other areas of the Midwest. Over time, the travelers grew weary of the commute and wanted more local meeting places. By the mid-'60's, there were conversations about forming ACG chapters outside New York.

Chicago launch: 1968

"In 1964, I moved to Chicago to become senior vice president of acquisitions at National Can Corp.," wrote Don Reed, a founding member of ACG Chicago. "I then began a more serious interest in ACG New York meetings. I became quite involved in the formation of a Chicago chapter, the first chapter outside of New York, and was its first president from 1968 to 1969."

Because of logistics and an identity with ACG and its career value, businessmen in other parts of North America started chapters closer to home. Over a period of five years, three chapters took shape—Chicago (1968), Toronto (1971), and Los Angeles (1972). With New York, these chapters laid the foundation for the ACG we know today.

"The Chicago chapter grew quickly, with early leaders including Fred Roberton, Tom Smith, James Ryan, Hugh Wagner, Ken Bony, Bill Howell, John Holmes, and many others that Tom, Fred, and I recruited," according to Mr. Reed.

Warner Rosenthal, who was vice president of corporate development for a division of Beatrice Foods at the time, attended the first meeting of ACG Chicago at the Ambassador East Hotel. Mr. Reed was in charge of the meeting, and Peter Hilton led the discussion, said Mr. Rosenthal. He described the event as "much more an after-work punch-and-cookies meeting with networking. The focus was on corporate members, but the service folks were the ones who attended." (Interestingly, this concern—maintaining a balance of corporate member and service provider so that all parties' interests are served by the organization—recurs through the next fifty years of the organization.)

The template for the ACG chapter meeting—a forum to exchange ideas, experiences, policies, and procedures, with guest speakers keynoting and offering larger viewpoints—was formed right away. "CEOs of large companies were invited to meetings and told war stories about mergers and acquisitions," said ACG pioneer Tom Smith, who was affiliated in the early '70s with Ernst & Ernst in Chicago. "Listeners would stand in line saying, 'Buy me,'" said Mr. Smith, who became the first president of ACG Global in 1972. He became a crusader for ACG with Mr. Hilton and others.

"Mr. Smith was an excellent organizer and recruiter," said Phil Nielsen of A.C. Nielsen Company. (Mr. Nielsen became ACG Global president in 1989 and was active in the Chicago chapter earlier like Mr. Smith.)

Recalled Jim Tucker, Spectral Dynamics, Inc., who as his career evolved became a member of ACG Orange County, "I joined ACG Chicago in the mid '70s, at the request of Tom Smith. Tom had arranged the deal for the first company I purchased, which was in Cincinnati. It created a long commute to meetings."

Toronto launch: 1971

Robert Coffey, who was working for Ernst & Ernst in Toronto, attributes the formation of the first Canadian chapter to the pioneering efforts of Messrs. Smith and Hilton.

"Toronto became the third chapter because Peter Hilton and Tom Smith wanted ACG to be international," said Mr. Coffey.

After a small planning meeting, Mr. Coffey helped corral 125 businessmen and women to the launch of ACG Toronto, where Messrs. Smith and Hilton "pumped up the crowd" to join ACG. Meeting attendance afterward hovered around eighty, said Mr. Coffey, who remained active in his home city but also became interested in the international organization and joined its leadership in the mid-'70s. Mr. Coffey chaired the InterGrowth conference in 1976 and took the reins as ACG Global president in 1978.

Los Angeles Launch: 1972

The first president of the Los Angeles chapter was John Castellucci, according to the 1972 InterGrowth brochure. Mr. Castellucci, employed by Cardiff Industries, quickly lost interest in ACG, and after his term moved away and "never showed up at an L.A. meeting again," recalled Paul Johnson of Hoover, Johnson & Company, who was president of the chapter in 1976.

John Heath, an executive with Marshall & Stevens, Inc., became the second president. He was followed by Neill Lawton, who had an MBA from Harvard and was manager of the industrial department of Security National Bank. Mr. Lawton's profession helped customers sell family-held businesses and find acquisitions. "Security [National Bank] was an outstanding group in Southern California prior to its acquisition by Bank of America," said Mr. Johnson, who served as Mr. Lawton's membership chairman.

In the late '70s, the chapter was considering dropping out of ACG to become a local association. "ACG did not seem to be worth the dues invested," according to Mr. Johnson. "ACG President Tony Hass [1975–76] came out to see us and convinced us to stay affiliated. It was after I started attending InterGrowth that the value of a national organization became more significant," he added.

By 1976, ACG Los Angeles had close to fifty members, half corporate and half service. Some companies were building conglomerate businesses, and private equity firms were just emerging.

"By intent the chapter grew slowly over the following years," said Mr. Johnson. "We worked hard at recruiting corporate executives and admitted only service members who had significant responsibility in their organizations and fit in with our group. We tried to avoid too much competition between service firms or accepting service members who would aggressively buttonhole corporate members for business purposes. We worked hard at maintaining good programs with educational value. We had a collegial atmosphere and thought our attendance was good," he added.

"During the early years, we had frequent visitors from San Francisco, San Diego, Phoenix, and other markets, some of which established new chapters," continued Mr. Johnson.

Howard Vultee of Merrill Lynch in San Francisco left the ACG Los

Angeles chapter to help establish the San Francisco chapter in 1976. Los Angeles members working or living in Orange County a few years later formed a chapter there in 1984. "We had some reservations about encouraging an Orange County chapter because it would cut into our membership, but we eventually encouraged it. That same year the San Diego chapter was formed," said Mr. Johnson.

He summarized, "Our chapter was small, collegiate, with low-key networking, which we called a social hour, and our Christmas party was held in someone's home."

The sense of intimacy would eventually change with the growth of the ACG InterGrowth conference. For several years conversations back and forth questioned whether it should be an exclusive club event or an explosive, all-encompassing opportunity for members to make deals.

Eventually the latter won out. But not at first.

CHAPTER 2

THE SEEDING OF INTERGROWTH

1972–1980
EXPANSION
Introduction and seeding of InterGrowth

With the 1970s the old aversion to lawsuits fell by the wayside.
It became easier to borrow money. Federal regulations were
relaxed. Markets became internationalized. Investors became
more aggressive, and the result was a boom in the number and
size of corporate takeovers.

— Malcolm Gladwell: Outliers

Enthusiasm for a conference that would bring together four hundred members and their spouses to socialize, learn, and network was confirmed by a member survey dispatched by the leadership in 1971. The outgrowth a year later, led by Fred Roberton of the Chicago chapter, was a conference called "InterGrowth"—a name "reflecting the inter-person, inter-company, inter-chapter and international character of the young organization," according to the conference brochure.

With international relations a focus from the beginning (reflecting a growing interest in offshore markets), ACG leaders chose Mexico City's Camino Royale Hotel—a four-star venue "complementing the standards established by the meeting accommodations of the Pierre (NYC) and Ambassador (Chicago) Hotels"—as the conference site. *(Note: An opportunity to stage the event in Portugal fell through because of logistical problems. Mexico City was actually a second choice.)*

Thirty-one members (7 percent of the membership), thirteen non-members, and thirty-two spouses and guests attended the first InterGrowth. Importantly, the organizers set a high bar by tapping influential business and political leaders as speechmakers. Peter Hilton offered an important talk on the value of acquiring spinoff companies, and Donald Rumsfeld, director of the US Office of Economic Development for President Richard Nixon, spoke. The US ambassador to Mexico, Robert McBride, turned up as a special guest. "I remember a private tour of the embassy for several of us," reminisced Donald Reed, with

The Reed Group of Florida and ACG president 1976–1977. *(A note in ACG archives states that Mr. Rumsfeld, who later became the US Secretary of Defense, did not accept reimbursement for the $24-per-night fee for two nights at InterGrowth, but instead paid the tab from his own pocket.)*

First InterGrowth 1972 held in Camino Real, Mexico City
(left to right) Caroll Greathouse (ACG Executive Director)
Unknown, Fred Roberton (ACG Global President 1975-75),
wife, Robert G. Coffey (ACG Toronto)

Building on the success of this meeting, ACG leaders determined quickly that InterGrowth would continue annually in select four-and five-star venues on alternating coasts of the United States. Planners were cautious about choosing another offshore site. "We recognized that the idea of offshore meetings caused some corporate shock," said Mr. Reed. "Several corporations felt it was bad practice for their officers to attend expensive offshore meetings when other staff could not do so as well."

They made an exception almost right away. "We did move it offshore several years later at the Southampton Princess in Bermuda," Mr. Reed added, but that would be the last overseas venture until EuroGrowth took place in London decades later.

Bob Coffey, with Ernst & Ernst and a founder of ACG Toronto, became chairman of the conference in Bermuda in 1975, the fourth InterGrowth. The trend to sign up "name speakers" continued. Victor Korn of Korn Ferry and Buzz McCormick took the podium. Volunteers were heavily involved. Mr. Coffey commented that he was able to run the conference by engaging his secretary from his office in Toronto to organize registration, presumably because the ACG management firm at the time, headed by Carroll Greathouse of Connecticut, did not have responsibility for full conference oversight. It would be several years before InterGrowth was managed by a professional staff, and volunteers like Mr. Coffey gave significant time and attention to make InterGrowth succeed.

Early ACG InterGrowth

Speakers, Networking, Parties, and Awards

From the first, InterGrowth's overriding objective was "to broaden the horizons of the executives engaged in internal, external, domestic and multi-national corporate growth," according to publicity brochures. It remained a three-day event with an evening reception kickoff for more than twenty-five years. Attendees—referenced as "husbands" in 1972—received binders with speeches and activity charts. Spouses—referenced as "wives" early on—enjoyed separate programming.

InterGrowth chairmen (and eventually-women) were selected for vision and leadership skills. Many later became ACG presidents. A variety of factors affected how the chair approached his or her job, but generally there was consensus about the theme from board members, who in turn would offer their support to ensure an exceptional event.

ACG Global Awards

First Institutional Award Given

At InterGrowth in 1975 in Bermuda, ACG assigned its first industry award named for ACG founder Peter Hilton. Mr. Hilton had died of complications from a bee-sting incident that occurred while he was gardening. As ACG's second president after Tom Smith, Mr. Hilton was respected as a creator, catalyst, author, and businessman. He was described by Mr. Smith as someone concerned "with all aspects of corporate growth—from product innovations to acquisitions, divestitures, and corporate diversification programs—throughout his life."

The criteria for the award, given in 1975 to Franklin Mint Company and awarded for thirty-four years subsequently, were straightforward— "an organization that has demonstrated outstanding growth performance with sales of $500 million or more."

(Note: In 1992, the Hilton Award was renamed The Founder's Award, and in 1996 renamed the Outstanding Corporate Growth Award. It was

disbanded at the global level in 2009 but continues to be awarded locally by many ACG chapters. Its criteria remain essentially the same.)

Thomas Smith, President ACG Global 1972-1973

Awards: Behind the Scenes

Eventually, after the first few awards were determined by ACG Global leaders, chapters got involved. At least in the '80s and perhaps before, nominations for the ACG Hilton Award bubbled up from the chapters, many of which began their own awards programs and submitted local winners for the global competition. It was an involved process, one that Warner Rosenthal of Beatrice Foods, for example, took seriously over many years for the Chicago chapter.

"The awards program at the chapter level was great," said Mr. Rosenthal. "It gave us the opportunity to evaluate local companies. We spent time comparing them statistically. Each committee member did his homework thoroughly and brought back information to the awards committee, which made the final selection. The drawback at the national level, when it selected from candidates supplied by many chapters, was that the president or CEO of the winning company was required to speak at InterGrowth. That could hamper the process."

Like the awards process, ACG chapters and membership were growing and adding to ACG's building reputation as a quality organization focused on middle-market mergers & acquisitions. By 1979, the association claimed twelve chapters and nearly sixteen hundred members. Things were revving up.

THE BLAZING '80s
Boom Time For M&A

The '80s were a boom time for M&A, pundits calling it a time of "merger mania." In the marketplace "The amount of money involved in M&A every year on Wall Street increased 2,000 percent—from the mid-1970s to the end of the 1980s—peaking at almost a quarter of a trillion dollars."

— Malcolm Gladwell: Outliers

Growth infused ACG, with much of the membership gain from service providers who were hunting and doing deals.

"The activity of our members made front-page news," said Gary Fiebert of Gilbert Tweed Associates, Inc., and ACG president from 1982–1983. "This fueled the growth of ACG with new members coming from corporations (principals), investment banks, financial institutions, accounting firms, appraisers, and consultants." The success of all kinds of acquisition bids—both solicited and increasingly unsolicited varieties—sharpened M&A skills and advanced professional opportunities up and down Wall Street and internationally.

ACG, though focused on the middle market, enjoyed the fruits of this trend and continued to engage flamboyant and top dealmakers to speak at InterGrowth conferences. In 1980, Dr. Armand Hammer of Occidental Petroleum issued stunning remarks from the podium.* Later in 1982, T. Boone Pickens, attorneys Joe Flom and Martin Lipton, Ted Turner of Turner Broadcasting, and Peter Grace, "the great 'conglomerateur' who piled company on company and turned W.R. Grace into a purveyor of everything from bull semen to grilled cheese sandwiches," according to *Fortune* magazine, addressed the InterGrowth audience.

Recalled Bill St. John, ACG executive director from April 1984 to May 1986, "What I remember is that it was an exciting time to be involved with ACG. I was in my early to mid-thirties, and ACG was made up of brilliant Wall Street merger folks ... many even younger than I!" Mr. St. John was employed by ACG's second management firm, Lurie-Murphy & Associates of Chicago.

"I remember when Ted Turner was our keynote speaker at InterGrowth in 1984," continued Mr. St. John. "I was at the hotel [Arizona Biltmore, Phoenix], getting ready to walk over to the InterGrowth chairman's suite for the reception. My phone rang and a voice said, 'Hi, Bill, this is Ted Turner. Can you meet me at my room and show me where the party is?' I also remember when Peter Grace was our keynoter [1983]. I was concerned that Mr. Grace was not in the ballroom when he was scheduled to speak in thirty minutes. Suddenly I heard a helicopter land behind the ballroom and out walked Peter Grace onto the stage! Typical ACG stuff!"

InterGrowth—Early Summary

East Coast, West Coast, and offshore twice, InterGrowth continued over the decades to get bigger (in numbers and dollars) and better, taking its pulse regularly through attendee surveys. That generally 10 percent of the membership attended for the first thirty years became a helpful statistic for InterGrowth planners but a puzzling reality for other leaders looking for a more substantial and global event. Low turnout may have contributed to an elitist reputation starting to crystallize around the conference and ACG that lasted for many years; it also reflected InterGrowth's high cost vis-à-vis value to members more locally focused.

Thanks to business interests around the world and his "citizen diplomacy," Hammer cultivated a wide network of friends and acquaintances. Late in life, he would brag that he had been the only man in history friendly with both Vladimir Lenin and Ronald Reagan.

ACG Growth Struggles

InterGrowth and Internationalism

Using InterGrowth as the "hook," ACG continued to seek international membership as M&A activity heated up offshore. Harry Fendrich, today of CAM Interests, Inc. and ACG president from 1983–84, recalled that InterGrowth in the early '80s was a global experience with representatives from Australia, Spain, South America, and UK taking part. But these folks did not join. By the mid-'80s—in 1985 exactly—ACG had 21 chapters and 2,275 members but just a handful from overseas.

"Corporations were becoming multi-national, and strengthening the ACG chapter 'confederacy' was an important focus of our international efforts as a board," said Mr. Fendrich, who served first as president of ACG New York before taking over the reins of the global group. "We worked to demonstrate value of the overall organization largely through the excellent speakers and programs at the InterGrowth conference wherever it was held."

International Soft Launch in Mexico, London

The Mexico chapter that was slated in 1980 never flourished. In 1985, ACG New York, ACG, and the British-American Chamber of Commerce collaborated to bring an ACG chapter to London. InterGrowth in 1986 in Scottsdale, Arizona, carried the theme, *Growth Strategies in an International Setting*, and a year later, July 1987 saw the first meeting of ACG in London. InterGrowth in '87 also looked globally with its focus on international acquisitions and divestitures through auction. But like Mexico, the London chapter never got off the ground. *(Unlike Mexico, however, a London chapter was reconstituted in 1999 and lasted for ten more years.)*

(In 1990, ACG hosted in London its first (and only) EuroGrowth conference, in hopes that it would become part of the annual schedule of events. Co-hosted with The Economist *magazine, the event was not well attended. It was never held again.)*

Internationalism was an aspiration but not yet a reality.

Award Program Expands

Meanwhile, on the North American front, awards to brilliant companies and those with star potential continued to interest ACG. Sensormatic in 1984 received the freshly conceived ACG Emerging Company Award. Criteria for this award were more detailed than those for the Peter Hilton Award and included sales of $250 million or less, three years of documented growth, the promise for future growth, and an interest in building the surrounding community through philanthropy or hands-on activity.

Emerging Company Award Created

The Emerging Company Award was given alongside the Peter Hilton/ Outstanding Growth award at InterGrowth for twenty-three years. Several of the small companies went on to achieve significant global footprints. Cisco Systems and Amgen, both winners of the Emerging Company Award in the '90s, collected the Outstanding Corporate Growth Award years later.

Eventually the Emerging Company Award followed the path of the Outstanding Growth Award, and after twenty-three years of dual residency at global and local levels, resides today—effective in 2009—exclusively with the chapters.

Deal-Making Tools Add Member Value

Directory of Members

More printed services became part of the membership package in the 1980s. The ACG Membership Directory, launched in 1978, was mentioned by Mr. Fendrich "as a useful tool for business deal contacts." The printed directory grew more robust and detailed over the years but, like all print data, was difficult to keep current before the Internet. Several addenda were published as members came on board or changed business locations, and it became a major project for multiple staff.

The Journal

Discussions for another member benefit in the form of a magazine began in 1983, but did not bear fruit until 1986. A year before Hunt Whitacre with RJR Nabisco became ACG Global president, ACG published the first issue of ***The Journal of Corporate Growth***.

Mr. Whitacre, active in ACG New York before becoming president of ACG in 1987, also belonged to the Financial Executives Institute, which published a sophisticated magazine he admired. The former InterGrowth chair wanted to know what "lay behind the resumes" of such celebrity speakers as Brian Little of Fortsman, Little, a well-regarded private equity firm then, and many of the other name speakers.

Mr. Whitacre championed *The Journal's* publication as an important member benefit.

Offered as "a periodic publication that included top presentations given by speakers at chapter events and at InterGrowth," *The Journal* pursued little advertising support and almost from the beginning operated in the red. This was overlooked because it was a new member benefit that leaders especially endorsed. However, a provision that speakers who were quoted had full rights to edit their material before publishing was a big hurdle to its publishing. Getting final approvals was "like pulling teeth," said Carl Wangman.

Nonetheless, *The Journal* lasted for six years over the span of three management companies. Mr. Wangman's firm, The Breeden Company, took over the management of ACG in 1985 after acquiring Lurie-Murphy & Associates that May. The Breeden Company, its successor firm, the Association Management Company, and *its* successor, The Center for Association Growth, oversaw publication of *The Journal* from 1986 to 1992. "It was an editorial struggle and questionable financial proposition all along," said Mr. Wangman.

The Late '80s

Whispers of Sponsorship ...

The late '80s laid the foundation for a new wave of growth and opportunity for ACG in the form of a sponsorship "explosion" and a strong management team.

Said Andy Rice, senior vice president, international business of The Jordan Company, "Jay Jordan, chairman and managing principal of The Jordan Company, was already a big supporter of ACG when I joined his firm in 1989. We continued to be a major sponsor of InterGrowth for more than ten years, starting with the opening Jordan Reception in 1992."

... Changeover of Staff

From 1986 through 1990, ACG's executive director, Jay Mommsen, Jr., of The Breeden Company focused his attentions on InterGrowth. He made sure that it thrived financially, educationally, and socially. In 1990, Carl Wangman, CEO of The Breeden Company, took over the reins as ACG's executive director. That same year, he sold The Breeden Company to The Association Management Center (AMC) in Skokie, Illinois. That merger turned out to be a one-year affiliation. In 1991, Mr. Wangman left AMC and took with him one client, ACG. ACG became the backbone of his new firm, The Center for Association Growth, or TCAG (tee-cagg), as it was nicknamed at the start.

But things were rocky at first.

CHAPTER 3

ENDINGS AND BEGINNINGS

1990–1999
MAGNIFICENT CHANGE

The 1990s began on troubled footing for ACG Global. There was debt for the first time, low appreciation from the chapters, a new management situation threatening a significant hoist in the annual fee, an InterGrowth conference that lost money, and a publication underfunded.

Phil Nielsen, who was senior level with the A.C. Nielsen Company and ACG president from 1989 to 1990, recalled the headquarters-chapter disconnect. "When I was president and even afterwards, I visited chapters to give a five-minute pitch for ACG International (sic) and realized the audience had no idea of the services provided. Chapter membership criteria varied, and dues were not uniformly collected." Mr. Nielsen said he envisioned that the national organization "could be the driving force for assembling best practices of the chapters and sharing them at regional meetings of chapter leaders."

Other leaders, notably Alan Gelband, Gelband & Co., Inc.; Ken Kovalcik, Arthur Anderson & Co.; and Rakesh Kaul, Fingerhut Corporation, also took the matter seriously and looked for solutions to salvage and—more importantly—make the national hub valuable to the array of twenty-three chapters that wanted something more.

Alan Gelband, ACG Global Chairman 1992-93, talks with
Gordon Binder, Chairman and CEO of Amgen

Mr. Gelband, president from March 1992 to March 1993, added detail about the financial plight of ACG. "At the InterGrowth of my presidency, we did not meet the minimum attendance guaranteed the hotel, which wanted to charge us $25,000. We didn't have $25,000, so we negotiated to schedule an upcoming InterGrowth at the hotel and were forgiven the debt. Over the prior several years, ACG had incurred some other significant deficits, and our capital account was close to $0. We had some serious budget issues."

The ACG president preceding Mr. Gelband, Ken Kovalcik (1990–91) was president when staff executive Carl Wangman became executive director. At the time, Mr. Wangman worked with The Association Management Company (AMC), based in Skokie, Illinois. AMC held the contractual arrangement with ACG, not Mr. Wangman.

In 1991, Mr. Wangman and AMC parted ways.

When AMC provided Messrs. Kovalcik and Gelband with a $200,000 budget proposal for FY1992–1993, the leaders began to look for new management. (Up to that point, the association had assumed that it would continue with a management fee of $80,000.) They looked to Mr. Wangman, who had launched his own firm, The Center for Association Growth, in 1991.

Explained Mr. Gelband, "We decided to look at other management companies. I interviewed a few and then had a meeting with Ken Kovalcik, who was a highly committed, knowledgeable former president. He and I agreed we had to do something dramatic to turn the finances around. We also both felt that Carl Wangman had done a great job while working for ACG, and we thought that we could work with him and his new organization.

Ken Kovalcik, ACG Global Chairman 1990-91

"One of the first things we did was to have a meeting with Carl at the 21 Club in New York," recalled Mr. Gelband. "At this meeting, Carl agreed to work for ACG for $80,000 plus incentives. His willingness to work for much less than his former employer was the first step to getting ACG on strong ground."

To gain the necessary financial footing, Mr. Gelband and his board made three key decisions that brought new financial security. They include:

1. **The launch of a sponsored opening reception at InterGrowth in 1992.** The decision by Jordan Industries and its sister company, The Jordan Company, to host this event provided a new venue and voice for service providers throughout ACG. Sponsorship would enable new and bigger conferences in chapters, and at InterGrowth it bolstered the deal-making community. "The Jordan Reception" would become a not-to-be-missed and must-be-seen-at event; it set a high bar for value.

The Jordan Influence

"Jay Jordan, who received ACG Chicago's Lifetime Achievement Award in 2010, was already a supporter of ACG when I joined the company in 1989," said Andy Rice, senior vice president, international business, and ACG Global chairman 2011–2012. *"Jay was a keynote speaker at InterGrowth several times and has spoken at chapter events—more than half in the US—and it is rumored that he has spoken at more ACG events nationwide than anyone else over the past twenty years."*

Alan Gelband, ACG Global Chairman 1992-93,
Jay Jordan, Jordan Industries, Andy Rice, Jordan Industries,
future ACG Global Chairman 2011-2012

2. **Employing a sales director** put the stake in the ground:
   sponsorship would be key to future planning of all ACG
   events. Someone with the assignment and right skill set
   would ensure the important revenue stream.
3. **The dissolution of** *The Journal for Corporate Growth,*
   a 100+ page magazine edited by Paul O. Gaddis of the
   University of Texas at Dallas. ACG's first attempt at
   printing and circulating intellectual capital, it had become
   a financial burden with less intellectual value because
   speakers heavily edited their remarks.

These factors simplified the decision to abandon it in 1992 and save
ACG $75,000 annually. "A politicized decision, but one easily reached
when we reviewed the numbers with the board," said Mr. Gelband.

Strategic Plan: Make First-Tier Organization

The sponsorship and publication decisions set ACG on a profitable
trajectory for the first time in two and a half years. "We had secured
the cash flow to finance growth initiatives stemming from the strategic
plan of 1990–1991," said Mr. Gelband.

Rakesh Kaul, an ACG director who was highly regarded for his professional work in strategic planning, led the process in Dallas, where seven directors and three staff gathered for two days. The theme was how to make ACG a first-tier organization.

What was necessary, according to the strategists, was a wide-ranging list of actions that advised the leaders to:

- **Develop a marketing strategy**
- **Stem the financial downturn**
- **Improve the loss/gain ratio of chapters, including international sites**
- **Centralize financial operations, administration of chapters and programming**
- **Develop an awards program recognizing service to ACG**
- **Review and improve the corporate/service member mix**
- **Make volunteers more strategic advisers and less hands-on specialists**
- **Launch a comprehensive skills database and ACG directory**
- **Institute a monthly newsletter**
- **Provide volunteer training**
- **Expand the membership to 3,500 by 1995**
- **Add to member value with new proprietary products— professional development programs, services, and recognition**

Mr. Kaul viewed the professional segmentation of ACG members as follows:

- **strategy—long-term owners who create synergistic value via business combinations**
- **finance—immediate owners to create value via liquidity and restructuring options**
- **facilitation—advisors who are involved, but not in the decision-making capacity**
- **'preneurs—new venture managers internally in the corporate entity or entrepreneurs externally**
- **ex's—individuals in transition who are looking to a position in any of the above four groups and initiate recommendations for responsive ACG-wide programs**

Said Mr. Nielsen, "The strategic plan gave structure … and opened

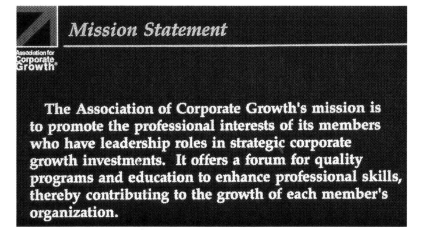

doors to a greater role for the staff and the central organization." Goals were prioritized at the strategy session, and an overall marketing-membership approach was identified: *Members were priority customers and should be treated as such.*

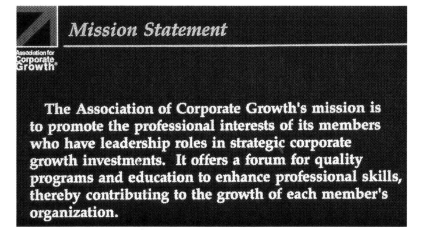

Mission Statement

Association for
Corporate
Growth®

The Association of Corporate Growth's mission is to promote the professional interests of its members who have leadership roles in strategic corporate growth investments. It offers a forum for quality programs and education to enhance professional skills, thereby contributing to the growth of each member's organization.

ACG Mission Statement 1991

Selling Chapters on Global Office First Meant Learning Their Needs

Introductions, Visits

During his presidency, Mr. Gelband wanted unity. "Like some of my predecessors, I decided to call each chapter president and discuss ACG locally and nationally. I visited a few chapters as well."

Mr. Gelband encountered problems. "The Boston and Arizona chapters wanted to disassociate with ACG, as they thought they realized no benefit from the national organization.

"We were fortunate that Russell Robb, of O'Conor Wright Wyman, Inc., was the president of the Boston chapter," continued Mr. Gelband. "A real turning point for ACG came at that first board meeting during my administration. Some previous ACG presidents attended. They argued that either we were going to be a local lunch club or a powerful international organization that would benefit all members. I think that Russ and all the other questioning people there started thinking positively about the value of ACG. Boston stayed a member and went on to become one of the largest chapters and contributors to the organization."

Commented Mr. Robb about the same incident, "The Boston chapter was insulated from ACG Global because few of us had ever been to InterGrowth. I'll never forget when I got a call from Alan one day in which he announced himself: 'Hi, I'm Alan Gelband!' I immediately said: 'Alan who? I've never heard of you.' Of course, he was the newly elected president of ACG Global."

Proactivity—Russ Robb and ACG Boston

"As president of the Boston chapter around 1990–1991, I went to a regional meeting in Newark in May. Charles Conner, Jr., of Bowles Hollowell Conner & Co., Burt Alimansky, of Alimansky Capital Group, Inc., and K. Clark Childers, of Offutt Childers & Putman, P.C., and other ACG luminaries were there," said Mr. Robb. "When it was my chance to talk about Boston, I passed out a program brochure complete with dates, places, speakers for the next twelve months. This really got Carl Wangman's attention, and I thought, *Well, hell, isn't this what a chapter president is supposed to do?* Boston was a restart chapter after being dormant for several years during the mid-1980s. So in order to build the membership, we decided on several important aspects during my tenure."

"Although we couldn't really afford it, we hired a professional administrator, Dee Calabrese.

"We really obtained the absolute best possible speakers in the Boston area—CEOs of well-known companies, leading venture capitalists, marquee names like Charles Connor from then the top investment bank, Bowles Hollowell & Conner ... all relevant to deal-making, M&A.

"We offered programs for eleven out of the twelve months.

"We had grass-roots solicitation for meetings and sent out faxes the day before as reminders.

"We organized a full-day seminar with keynote speaker Lester Thurow of MIT, who had just written a bestselling book on the three leading economies—Europe, USA, and Japan. We didn't pay Lester, who was a prestigious draw, but we bought two hundred of his books.

"We expanded the board, made them work, and rotated the president every year to spread around the enthusiasm.

"We went to InterGrowth for the first time and really were drawn in by Carl's group, The Center for Association Growth, so we came away hyped up about the organization.

"We kept the costs affordable and screened out non-M&A types who wanted to join for purely networking.

"We set up a breakfast group, called 'Buyouts Breakfast,' of just private equity groups with speakers eleven months of the year, fifteen miles outside Boston, next to the highway. Service providers were not invited. We had thirty attendees compared to the larger luncheons of one hundred-plus attendees.

"We injected a feeling of excitement and camaraderie within the group."

Regional Chapter Leadership Meetings Aid Understanding

In early 1992, prompted by the disparity between chapters and need for greater understanding between all parties, ACG Global leadership began a series of regional meetings with chapter leaders throughout the United States. The meetings brought together leaders from five or six chapters to a regionally suitable location and were chaired by the ACG president and Mr. Wangman. Their purpose was to share best practices and bridge any communication gap between the chapters and ACG Global. Their value grew as they became more focused and well attended.*

McGrath Years: Data Dictates Direction

The flourishing chapter in Boston was not lost on Ed McGrath, ACG Global president from 1993–1994. Mr. McGrath, executive director of CAMA, Inc., emphasized chapter viability and building the prestige of ACG. Noted for scrupulous membership/chapter data analysis and hopeful, "sky-is-the-limit for ACG" thinking, Mr. McGrath wanted the global hub to fortify local chapter success. He thought ACG's best role would fuel membership, bring national visibility to the organization, and make possible the sharing of intellectual capital among members. He attended to struggling chapters by visiting with their leadership and committing to help with their development. His ongoing cost-benefit analysis showed that successful chapters sustained at least eighty members, and he worked to help make that happen. His membership goal for ACG was 2,400 in 1994, which was exceeded by 500 members.

In 2011, Leslie Whittet, ACG Global vice president of chapter operations in 2011, observed, "Regional chapter leadership meetings are still key today. We invite four people per chapter, and 80 percent of all the chapters in the six regions in ACG today participate."

InterGrowth: Elitism, Networking, or Both

As other presidents of ACG showed concern about the disconnect between ACG Global and the chapters, Mr. McGrath focused on a disconnect between InterGrowth and the mission and purposes of ACG. He saw the discrepancy clearly while serving as InterGrowth chair in 1991, one year before he became president.

He wrote, "I believe there was a profound transition in ACG at the time I was on the board. Before that time, there was an 'elitist' atmosphere or character to the membership. It seemed epitomized by the restrictive membership standards." This opinion was influenced by his own experience: it had taken Mr. McGrath three years to become an ACG San Francisco member, despite the fact that he had attended several InterGrowths and was friends with many people on the board of directors.

Notwithstanding Mr. McGrath's desire to eschew ACG's elitism, ACG InterGrowth meetings continued to have an elitist appeal, tagged as "discerning and sophisticated." This was reinforced by the world-class venues in Florida, Arizona, and California and the annual palette of successfully renowned speakers that nonetheless attracted a small portion of the membership, still about 10 percent.

The five-star InterGrowth attraction was a successful economic venture for eighteen years until 1991. But the year Mr. McGrath chaired—at the Boca Raton Resort and Club—the event lost money, due in part by the slowing economy and an unpopular Middle East war.

He rued the fact that he may have been the first chair to post a negative return from InterGrowth.

Look Ahead Falls Short

Take-Home Value Lacking, Say Attendees

The next year at the Scottsdale Princess, InterGrowth planners focused on the future—"Strategies Beyond 2000" was the theme. Chair Tom Corrigan of G.E. Capital promoted the conference, "[We] will hit head-on the unprecedented changes confronting nearly all industries and the challenges that are being made to the very foundation of our business and social structures. This event will help you decipher the great global transformation in business today occurring on a scale not seen since the Industrial Revolution more than a century ago.

"We are honored to have a conference program of presentations by speakers and panelists who represent many of the most influential and interesting companies in the nation. They will share with us the future vision of the industry or constituents that they represent."

Mr. Corrigan followed through. Among the presenters were Don Reynolds of 21st Century Forecasting, Consuelo Mack from the *Wall Street Journal Report on Television,* Don Holt of *Fortune* magazine, and Paul Maidment of *The Economist.* Larry Smart from the National Center for Supercomputing Applications, Donald Soderquist of Wal-Mart stores, and Richard J. Riordan, who became mayor of Los Angeles the following year and served until 2001, presented. Also speaking were Albert Shanker of the American Federation of Teachers and George M.C. Fisher, CEO and chairman of Motorola. Many of their topics hit a futuristic theme.

Despite their luminescence, the visionaries did not sell. Attendees, who did not turn out in the numbers expected or budgeted for, criticized the InterGrowth program for its "lack of real take-home value." One evaluation that mirrored many others read, "I realize the importance of looking to the future, but our current economy and business conditions mandate more meat to help my business now."

InterGrowth Returns to Basics

The reaction in 1993 may have been predictable. InterGrowth's first woman chair, Patricia Buus, of the Lethridge Group in Chicago, heard the outcry from attendees of the prior InterGrowth and developed a program focused on basics. Promotional materials ascribed to her the following sentiments, "No one needs to tell us that 'business as usual' is dead and that many of the plans and programs of the '80s are inadequate for the '90s. We live with this sense of urgency every day. We know our mandate is to do more with less NOW!"

Basics Spurs New Programming: The Deal—Front and Center

Under the Buus leadership, InterGrowth at the Hyatt Regency Grand Cypress in Orlando, Florida, carried out its *Doing More with Less: Corporate Growth Today* theme with a black-and-white brochure to downplay the five-star backdrop and emphasize the "back-to-basics" education. The belt-tightening approach spawned significant new products:

"Breakfast Roundtable" discussions on deals and the market carried a variety of timely themes that members discussed in small units. These were conducted by Jim Blaha of Business Appraisal Company (BAC) from the Chicago area. Attendees awoke early to participate.

The "Deal Mart," an hour-long program that allowed members one minute to tell the InterGrowth audience about a deal, also launched in 1993. It was an overnight hit—sold out and well attended. The key was the opportunity to verbalize a deal possibility in front of the poised InterGrowth audience. Some would say that Deal Mart laid seeds for the ACG Capital Connections a decade later.*

Note: Deal Mart would expand to a two-hour exchange the following year and fueled a new "Dealmaker's Exchange" in 1994, essentially a second opportunity for ACG sellers and buyers to share information with tables that sold for $1,000 apiece.

In 1997, Dealmaker's Exchange had featured billing as the half-day event that kicked off the conference. The name was shortened to "Deal Exchange" and described as a showcase of prospective deals.

Deal Mart, Dealmaker's Exchange, and Deal Exchange may have laid the seeds for a more robust tradeshow that became known several years later as "PEG Marketplace" (in Los Angeles) and "ACG Capital Connection" (in Boston). From its beginning in 1993 and through all its iterations, the showcase for deal-making—ACG Capital Connection, as it was branded in 2004—was a hit and a money-maker for ACG.

Two Times in Three Years

In 1994, ACG InterGrowth returned to the Scottsdale Princess. Selecting the same venue twice in three years was unprecedented in InterGrowth history. However, when the 1992 InterGrowth at the Scottsdale Princess fell short of projections for room revenue, ACG ducked the $25,000 penalty by promising to return two years later.

Jim Bondoux of The Fremont Group described his approach as InterGrowth chair in 1994 as deal-rich and sized just right.

"I elected to use the deal contacts to highlight the key issues of corporate growth… One of the reasons InterGrowth attracts so many repeat attendees is that the gathering is just the right size—small enough for finding and renewing acquaintances and large enough to make new contacts. The flavor is almost that of an informal club, one that binds its members more intimately than do most professional associations. You'll find an atmosphere of warm friendliness balances the intensity of the program," said Mr. Bondoux, hovering on the elitism aspect eschewed by Mr. McGrath and Ms. Buus just a few years before.

Reflecting ACG's desire to increase attendance, room rates were lower than the previous year, and registration fees were rolled back to 1988 levels. The decisions worked; InterGrowth attendance hit a record that year and contributed to the association's surplus.

MAGNIFICENT CHANGE
PART 2: 1994–2000

Back on the Ranch—Global Focus Returns; Private Equity, Diversity, and Worldwide Web Show Up

Russ Warren's presidency from 1994–1995 came after many years of his activity in chapters, including New York and Cleveland, which he helped found. Then president of The TransAction Group (which later became part of Edgepoint Capital Advisors), Mr. Warren said, "In 1995, ACG was financially sound and growing in members. We decided to align it with three long-term mega-trends observable in business:

1. Increasing globalization of middle market businesses in many sectors and OEMs winnowing suppliers to companies with critical mass
2. Rise of private equity firms, which provided an orderly market for owners seeking a liquidity event, and
3. Greater diversity in business leadership."

Consequently Mr. Warren and the ACG boards that followed afterward:

1. Ramped-up efforts to extend beyond North America **by expanding the role of vice president of international expansion.** *The process culminated in 1999 under the leadership of Vice President of International Expansion Charlie Downer of Downer and Company, who crafted the reboot of the London chapter (or the "Corporate Development Association" as it was called then).*
2. Recommended a **private equity category** of membership and developed programming to reflect their interests. *In 1998, under Charles Conner's presidency, the new member*

category Private Equity Group became an official ACG designation.

3. Recommended that Diane Harris of Bausch and Lomb in Rochester, New York, become the **first female president** of ACG, *which occurred in 1997, a few years after Mr. Warren's recommendation.*

Another cutting-edge decision of Mr. Warren's, which followed the strong recommendation of the Boston chapter, was to hire a professional administrator for ACG Cleveland. Joan McCarthy, founder of MJM Services, Inc., assumed the role in 1987.

Joan McCarthy continues to hold the office of ACG executive in 2011. In addition to ongoing administration of a growing chapter, she and her staff launched ACG Cleveland's Annual Dealmaker's Awards Program in 1995, one of the chapter's most successful events still today.

Ms. McCarthy's leadership in ACG also included many years of involvement at InterGrowth where she, Pat Pickford of ACG San Francisco, and Judy Taylor of ACG St. Louis formed a core team that managed registration and built enduring regard from attendees. "Low tech, high touch" was their successful delivery method. Ms. McCarthy received in 2010 the first ACG President's Award at InterGrowth in Miami, Florida, for outstanding service to ACG.

ACG Newsletter, Marketing Program Launched

Also under Mr. Warren's reign, TCAG brought in a marketing director to lead the program. Under Judy Iacuzzi's leadership, one of the first initiatives of Iacuzzi Associates, Inc. was to create a monthly newsletter conveying highlights of chapter life and ACG thought leadership. *ACG Network*, which was published ten years, sought advertising from the get-go but did not become a profitable venture. It would, however, lead the way to greater internal examination and communication and new external products that garnered national media attention.

Collateral materials for membership, the Corporate Development Conference, and sponsorship were new marketing tools developed right away. Membership brochures, tailored to chapter needs for corporate/ service and private equity members, were distributed to all chapters at no cost.

ACG started to pay systematic attention to the media. Press releases related to InterGrowth and ACG awards—Outstanding Growth, Emerging Company, and Meritorious Service—were dispatched locally and nationally starting in 1995.

Ramping up Research

ACG's marketing committee decided to ask InterGrowth attendees to complete a survey about business opportunity and the economic climate. The results were tabulated and published in *ACG Network,* the monthly newsletter.

Successive surveys tracked the issues on the minds of dealmakers at the time. In 1995, the survey asked respondents to value various influences on the deal marketplace, such as: shareholder value, innovation, international competition, government debt, productivity, adequate ROI, growth factors, skilled employees, government regulation, tax reform, pricing pressures, health costs, environmental liabilities, restructuring, cost of raw materials, and funding sources.

These ACG industry surveys were prepared and distributed to the InterGrowth audience for four years. When e-mail gained widespread support at the end of the century, the surveys were refined and delivered electronically to all members; annual became semi-annual.

In 1998, ACG outsourced some of the public relations work to the Financial Relations Board (FRB), which used the industry surveys as a basis for more widespread publicity. One of FRB's brilliant successes came at InterGrowth in 1999 in Palm Springs, California. The *Wall Street Journal* announced in a small, front-page, boxed story, "Deal-A-Minute," a reference to InterGrowth's Deal Exchange happening that very morning. FRB also mounted the first two New York media tours for ACG Presidents Conrad Tuerk in 1999 and Chris Gebelein in 2000.

ACG's first five-minute video showcasing InterGrowth's value was filmed in 1995 at The Breakers in Palm Beach, Florida. Recognizing nearly twenty-five years of InterGrowth, the highlight video was used as a promotional tool by the chapters to ramp up interest in InterGrowth the following few years.

Membership Growth Focus Continued

The administrations of Bill Killian (1995–1996), vice president of Johnson Controls, Inc., and Larry Roberts (1996–1997), founder of Technology Strategies & Alliances of Menlo Park, California, continued to emphasize membership growth ("... *achieve total membership of 4,000 by June 1997 and 5,000 by June 2000, and 10,000 by 2010,*" according to board meeting minutes,) through new chapters ("... *have 40 US chapters by June 2000*") and international expansion ("... *have two Canadian chapters by 1998 and one Mexican chapter by 1998*"). Messrs. Killian and Roberts's administrations revitalized a strategic plan that led to new goals of chapter and international expansion and increasing financial stability.

Mr. Killian was a twenty-year ACG veteran who helped launch the Detroit and Wisconsin chapters. With Johnson Controls, he had abundant experience working in European mergers and acquisitions and corporate development markets. Mr. Killian appointed as his ACG vice president of international expansion Diane Harris, an international veteran and leading dealmaker for Bausch & Lomb as vice president of corporate development. Ms. Harris and her international vice-presidential successor, David Love of Ray & Berndtson, laid the groundwork for the launch of several European chapters.

Another Killian-Roberts goal to increase corporate membership and participation in ACG led to new programming and leadership. Ms. Harris was particularly influential in this regard. Her systematic analysis of the corporate development role was informed by a survey tool she created and dispatched to ACG corporate members over a period of years. It posed gritty questions about responsibility levels, "pecking order," and compensation. These led to ACG conferences for corporate members only.

Mr. Killian's administration underwrote the first of four ACG Corporate Development Conferences attended by strategic (corporate) officers from North America. Three more would take place, two in New York and one in Washington, DC, before the turn of the century. Eventually the one- or one-and-one-half-day event, which never achieved profitability, morphed into an exclusive Corporate Development education track at InterGrowth in 1999.

Texas InterGrowth: A Highlight of Larry Roberts's Presidency as written by Mr. Roberts:

In my recollection, the most pivotal year was the year prior to my presidency when Bill Killian was president and I was president-elect. During that time, and on the day that the O.J. Simpson decision was announced, Bill and I holed up in a hotel room in Atlanta area and drafted what would become the five-year strategic plan later adopted by the board.

We agreed to try a Texas location at Hyatt Regency Hill Country Hotel in San Antonio for InterGrowth, a roaring success ...

I was part of a team that recommended Diane Harris as my successor, our first female president ...

We had an excellent board that year, including the chapter president members, a factor that enabled us to identify up-and-coming leadership at the chapter level. The board was independent but not fractious."

Chapter Issues and Advancements in Mid–1990s

Foundering Relationship with Arizona, Atlanta; Seeding Seattle

Before taking office, Bill Killian and Larry Roberts together visited chapters in Arizona and Atlanta. They succeeded in "saving" Atlanta and losing Arizona. Recalled Mr. Roberts, "In retrospect, we had no chance in Arizona, which never found value in its connection to ACG Global. In the case of Atlanta, we accommodated its chapter invoicing practices, and the chapter has been a stalwart chapter ever since. Carl Wangman and I worked hard to get a Seattle chapter created, an endeavor that took five years to take root in 2001." *(Note: ACG Atlanta registered more than five hundred members in 2010.)*

In Boston, a new Buyouts Roundtable meeting construct delivered a private equity exchange on the outskirts of the city over breakfast rather than lunch or evening. Attendance built swiftly.

The successful program developments in Boston caught the attention of other chapters—large and small—that began adding new formats and times to the established monthly lunch meeting slate. These changes typically began mid-decade: half-day seminars, co-branded meetings with like-minded organizations, or breakfasts on the periphery of town. Accommodating professional interests and logistical demands of a diverse membership—private equity members were being tagged as a budding membership group, for example—changed the configuration of ACG programming forever. That sponsorship was catching hold throughout the organization gave important grist to the expanded and imaginative activity.

Regional Conferences with Neighboring Chapters Catch Hold

While president of the Los Angeles chapter in 1991, Franz von Bradsky of Green Tree Capital, Inc. and Jim Mahoney of Mahoney & Company, Inc., (posthumous winner of the ACG Meritorious Service Award in 1993) organized the first ACG West Coast conference in Southern California. This included recruiting leadership of the San Diego, Orange County, and San Francisco chapters as participants and planners. The effort was a success, and set a precedent for ACG.

"Franz was also key in the transformation of the San Francisco chapter when he led the chapter's first major conference in the mid-'90s, 'Wall Street to Main Street,'" said Pat Pickford, veteran administrator of ACG San Francisco for sixteen years.

Several other ACG chapters realized they could sponsor regional conferences to great advantage. With it, they would leverage attendee size to engage major sponsorship, hear dazzling speakers, and attract first-tier business media. Starting in California, these regional events became part of the ACG fabric and flourished in major US markets (Dallas, Houston, Austin, New York/New Jersey/Connecticut, and others) by the turn of the twenty-first century.

Carl Wangman, ACG Executive Director, Tom Doyal, First President
ACG West Michigan, Rand Sobczak, President ACG Detroit 1999

1997: Communications Tipping Point

Launch of the first home page, precursor to the website

Diane Harris, president of ACG from 1997–1998, offered a V-I-S-I-O-N for ACG that stood for Value, InterGrowth, Strategic Plan Linkage, International Expansion, Online, and New Members and Chapters. Using this platform, Ms. Harris ramped up efforts for member-to-member communication and online activity, which she saw as an important tool to the accomplishment of the give-and-take. ACG's first home page launched under her watch even though only 15 percent of the membership at the time used e-mail. She also moved for the first online seminar (predating webinars) for members and authorities in the field to communicate "live" via telephone.

Said Ms. Harris, "We did not listen to the naysayers who did not use the Internet, but proceeded to develop the Internet capabilities in ACG, with George Gingerelli, who was experienced and saw the importance, leading the way.

"We reached out to corporate development officers who were not able to travel as freely as some of the service providers in ACG, starting with the Corporate Development Conference and chat rooms on the Internet.

"We were conscious of maintaining the balance of corporates to other members. We encouraged ACG to divide membership into more specific categories of accountants, lawyers, intermediaries (rather than lumping them into category of "service providers") so the mix would be more balanced. We published a resource directory of members willing to share best practices. I was called upon and I called upon others using that book.

"The other focus of significance was developing the international arm of ACG," said Ms. Harris, whose professional work with Bausch & Lomb gave her familiarity with European business development and lent muscle to the ACG UK campaign that bore fruit in 1999. She encouraged the spadework of successive ACG international affairs officers who eventually launched ACG Austria, ACG France, and ACG Holland.

A key player "on the ground" in the development of the organizing committees for the European chapters was long-time InterGrowth attendee Harald Klien of CDI Beteiligungsberatung in Vienna, Austria. He attended meetings in Frankfurt as early as 1995 and subsequently, in London, Amsterdam, Dusseldorf, and his home chapter of ACG Austria.

"I thought, *why not a chapter in Austria?*" said Mr. Klien recently, recalling the organizing days. "I collected five of my closest buddies then, and the group has controlled ACG Austria ever since." Mr. Klien's company administers the ACG Austria chapter, which meets quarterly.

"As a tribute to the US members, ACG Austria always has turkey at its fall meeting. If they cannot shoot turkeys, they disguise some other bird … maybe a pigeon!" he added, laughing.

Harald Klien, Co-Founder ACG Austria

ACG and UK on the Horizon—Again

ACG's enduring interest in the international marketplace began in Toronto. In the 1980s, chapters in London and Mexico City were seeded, but neither thrived. The Journal for Corporate Growth for winter 1991 Vol. 7 devoted its entire contents to the presentations at EuroGrowth (co-sponsored by ACG and Business International Ltd., the wing of The Economist that handled events and seminars). EuroGrowth took place in London in 1990. It whetted ACG's insatiable appetite for internationalism. And in the mid-'90s, the board created the position of vice president of international expansion and asked David Love to assume the post.

A string of ACG members, among them André Baladi of André Baladi & Associates and co-founder of the International Corporate Governance Network, Debbie Victory, of the Akron (Ohio) Regional Development Board, Ashley Rountree of Downer & Company, and Mrs. Harris, helped Mr. Love. All worked to secure greater exposure internationally—emphasis on Europe—with personal visits, lunches, and dinners overseas.

The spadework in the UK early in the decade brought fruit in the late 1990s. With the help of ACG member Charlie Downer, CEO of Downer & Co., ACG made contact with a leading corporate development officer at Smiths Industries. Robin Taunt was a highly regarded ACG member who often attended InterGrowth. With the leadership of these two individuals, the London chapter was reborn under the name Corporate Development Association in 1999. (Five years later, its leaders would change the name to ACG UK at the aegis of ACG's branding process to conform to the nomenclature of all other chapters.)

The chapter did not follow North American chapters with meeting diversity. Instead, ACG UK members met over lunch quarterly in one venue, offered a distinguished speaker or two such as The Right Honorable Kenneth Clarke, a conservative member of Parliament. The UK chapter was heavily corporate in membership makeup.

Interestingly, in 2010, Mr. Clarke was appointed by Prime Minister David Cameron to the British Cabinet as Lord Chancellor and Secretary of State for Justice. His famously pro-European integration views have often conflicted with the Conservative Party's skepticism of the EU.

EuroGrowth-London 1990

ACG Home Page and Internet Development

Growth under Harris and Gingerelli

George Gingerelli, vice president of communications and online services for four years, oversaw the launch of the ACG home page in 1996 and its expansion to a website at www.acg.org, officially announced in 2000. His correspondence to the board over the years conveys a vision to "be the number one location for information related to corporate growth," and offers pages of insightful detail of how to get there through design, content, and technology.

Mr. Gingerelli encouraged TCAG to partner with American Eagle, Inc., to host the ACG Global and chapter sites. ACG was one of the first customers of American Eagle, a start-up in 1996. Mr. Gingerelli's enthusiasm and cutting-edge understanding of what the World Wide Web could do for ACG got the board enthused. By the turn of the century, Mr. Gingerelli's plans were taking cyber shape. He wrote:

"An indication of the appeal of the revised www.acg.org is the number of 'hits' and 'visitor sessions' that the site experiences each month. In September of 1999, there were over 98,000 hits and about 7,000 sessions recorded. That was then, this is now. With more than 500,000 hits in August 2000 and nearly 2,000,000 hits in September 2000, it appears that our website is attracting interest. More importantly, visitor sessions increased to nearly 14,000 in August and 15,000 last month, exceeding the goal that we established last year. Here again, the true measure will be our ability to maintain and increase this level of interest."

Mr. Gingerelli envisioned a robust site that would pay for itself, build the brand, and entice new membership.

"Our website has enormous potential. As interest in the site grows, revenue from advertising and online transactions should become easier to achieve. Similarly, as a highly valued benefit of membership, the website can be used as a recruiting tool. Finally, operating the premier location on the Internet for online information and communication related to corporate growth should add significantly to the prestige of ACG Global," wrote Mr. Gingerelli in a memorandum to the board in 2000.

Tweaking the website, encouraging chapters to launch their own websites, gathering statistics on the success of these efforts, amending budgets to accommodate the venture, and communicating advances and changes to the entire organization via e-mail were sea changes in operations that kept staff and volunteers working hard and long … and faster than ever before.

Membership Growth Looks to Private Equity Groups

Following Ms. Harris' lead of differentiation between various services provided by members, her presidential successor, Charles Conner, wanted to entrench the private equity member (PEG) in particular. Heretofore, PEGs were intermixed with service providers—accountants, lawyers, etc. Mr. Conner, a partner with the Charlotte-based investment banking firm of Bowles Hollowell Conner, lobbied hard for a new member category—and won. Perhaps he foresaw, along with his board, that the private equity membership could become the deal-making backbone of ACG.

Said member Jay Jester, who at the time worked with Bowles Hollowell, "I remember Charles [Conner] taking some heat from the other senior guys for how much time he was spending on this small networking organization. BHC had built a very strong mid-market brand out of their offices in Charlotte. To my recollection, Charles was one of the first to push adding PEGs to the group of core ACG members. I very clearly remember Charles's leadership in this role (1998–1999), and how generously he used the strength of his personal brand and his firm's brand to bring credibility to this nascent effort."

Conrad Tuerk, President 1999–2000, Seals London Deal

The first ACG spokesman to agree to a whirlwind media tour in New York, Connie Tuerk of Tuerk and Associates, recalled, "… the most dramatic external factors in my long time at ACG were the ascent of the private equity industry and the globalization of the M&A business."

He added, "The major event in my term was to officially welcome the London branch to the ACG family, an event that truly made ACG an international organization. The meeting at The East India Club was special as was the whole trip with Janice and Carl [Wangman].

"Another event that made a great impression on me," continued Mr. Tuerk, "was when I chaired InterGrowth. Shortly before the event, our lead speaker, Al 'Chainsaw' Dunlap, backed out as he was about to be indicted for 'cooking the books' at Sunbeam Corp. I put out some frantic feelers to some of the more active ACG members and got instant response and an excellent substitute speaker.

"That really emphasized to me that some very busy and important people really cared about ACG, and it made me even more proud to be able to play a leadership role in the group."

Decade Wrap-Up

As the twenty-first century began, ACG leaders took stock of the significant milestones from the 1990s.

- The association committed itself to formalized strategic planning in 1991 and updated its strategic direction again in 1995.

- The association weathered a major financial crisis; staff leadership, headed by Carl Wangman at The Center for Association Growth, offered a steadying influence.

- ACG InterGrowth again became a profitable educational and networking event after its low point in the early 1990s. The dramatic increase in sponsorship dollars led in part by The Jordan Company, resulted in ACG's InterGrowth being a major contributor to the net profit of ACG Global.

- Eleven new chapters were added to the roster, including one in the United Kingdom, bringing the total number of chapters to thirty-four in 2000.

- The membership doubled from 2,544 members in December 1990 to over 5,000 in the millennium year.

- ACG chapters discovered the strategic benefits of diversifying their meeting schedules to accommodate widespread and focused members.

- ACG chapters developed the first collaborative programming with other chapters and like-minded organizations.

- ACG marketing endeavors became a priority; a vice president of marketing position was created on the board, and marketing and public relations consultants brought new communications tools and visibility to the association.

- The first ACG home page became an ACG website with the insight and direction of Diane Harris and George Gingerelli.

- The private equity industry gained greater recognition in the mid-1990s. Its importance was heralded by ACG presidents Russ Warren and Diane Harris, and was formalized in the ACG constituency by Charles Conner.

- Spotlighting the deal—by carving out solo events for dealmakers to exchange information—was first done at InterGrowth in 1993.

- The ACG Global board added a vice president for international expansion position, indicating a firmer commitment to international membership.

- Diane Harris became the first woman president in 1997.

- A vice president of corporate member affairs position was added to the ACG board of directors in 1995.

- Patricia Buus became the first woman to chair InterGrowth in 1993.

CHAPTER 4

CHANGES IN THE AIR

TWENTY-FIRST CENTURY
BEST-KEPT SECRET NO LONGER

John Gullman of Corporate Finance Partners chaired InterGrowth in 2000 and recalled immediate challenges facing ACG.

"InterGrowth was suffering a letdown, and we were looking to trim budgets. We discovered chapters like ACG Los Angeles and ACG Boston were conducting major events with budgets for speakers that exceeded those of InterGrowth.

"I encouraged ACG President Chris Gebelein of Borg Warner to re-establish formal strategic planning for the organization. I also thought that the idea to survey the members was a good idea. We did lots of business surveys over the years, but I did not remember ever asking the members what they thought or needed from ACG in a systematic way."

First Member-Needs Survey Leads to New Strategic Plan

ACG's first systematic member-needs research in June 2001 consisted of an online survey sent to about fifty-five hundred members and in-depth telephone interviews with twenty-four global directors, fifteen chapter leaders, five chapter executives (called *administrators* at the time), and four members of the global staff. Mr. Wangman and ACG Boston member Laura Matz of Hillcrest Associates, Inc., who headed the project, selected the interview candidates to ensure balanced feedback and diversity of ACG experience, geography, and viewpoint. The project ran over five months.

Results, shared throughout ACG in October 2001, became the foundation for a strategic planning session that followed. Key research findings included:

- ACG is generally perceived as local.
- Networking is the key reason for joining ACG.
- ACG needs to sharpen awareness through advanced public relations.
- The ACG Global board should help build awareness of ACG to a greater extent.

- The board should be more representative of the chapters.

The global board took the survey results seriously. Late in 2001, a strategic planning session, led by ACG member Craig Stokely of The Stokely Partnership, brought clear focus to the need for increased chapter support, public relations, and more. One of the first outcomes of the strategic plan was the establishment of a chapter support team of a wide range of volunteers and the entire global staff. It also led to other initiatives; the new strategies, goals, and actions follow.

1. Form a Global Chapter Support Team

Goal: To provide the tools necessary for chapter leaders to enhance the awareness of ACG and its value in the local market.

Actions:

(a) Create an ACG Vice President of Chapter Support position to provide service, quality control, and a mentorship program. This individual works with a total staff team to administer to each chapter's strength. *Note: This program was much more robust than in the past. It involved a total board/staff endeavor. Consisting of regular communication and reporting back and forth, it was an attempt to understand fundamental and differing needs and share best practices. (Continues in some form in 2011.) Key players: Leslie Whittet, Paul Stewart, Don Feldmann, Tom Doyal.*

(b) Bring together chapter administrators to network and share best practices. *Note: First Chapter Administrators Meeting in Chicago 2002. (Continues under new name, Chapter Executives Meeting in 2011.)*

2. Build the Brand

Goal: To establish ACG as the premier educational, social/networking, and professional member organization involved with corporate growth worldwide.

Action: Allocate resources to review and develop the ACG brand with a new design and a systematic plan of development and dispatch. *Note: Never before was the ACG brand handled in a systematic and cohesive way. ACG board members, chapters, and staff were part of the step-by-step process during 2002–2004 costing $250,000. Led by Patrick Hurley, ACG VP of*

Marketing, Dave Studeman of Landor Associates and Grey Ghost, Inc., and Bill Haynes of Magnet Communications. Other key players: Charlie Downer, Paul Stewart, Hazel Mack, Renate Herbst, and a dozen members of the brand task force.

3. Explain it, Network It

Goal (a): To communicate membership best practices throughout chapters by providing multiple platforms for networking among chapters and their members.

Action: Increase chapter leaders' attendance at InterGrowth by 100 percent in 2002, and increase total member attendance at InterGrowth by 10 percent per year, with a goal of 15 percent of the total membership attending.

Goal (b): To share best networking practices.

Action: Provide strategic planning survey results to chapter leaders; survey chapters by e-mail and phone to determine best networking practices and share results with chapter leaders; include networking best practices on agenda at regional chapter leadership meetings and at chapter leadership meeting at InterGrowth.

Goal (c): Improve regional networking among members.

Action: Develop new platforms to facilitate regional networking in areas where none exists; could include one-day regional conferences.

Note: An example of a local practice being shared throughout the organization to the ultimate benefit of all, PEG Marketplace—the forerunner of ACG Capital Connection— stands out as among the best. Introduced in ACG Los Angeles in 2002, it was a significant success; rolled out to entire InterGrowth audience in 2003, a continuing dramatic success. It was renamed ACG Capital Connection during the branding process. By 2005, eleven chapters sponsored an ACG Capital Connection; by 2010, twenty-two ACG Capital Connections were held. The events have universally accrued ACG and its chapters financial, member satisfaction, and public relations benefits for nearly a decade.

Goal (d): Communicate to external audiences.

Action (1): Build relationships with key press: *American City Business Journals (2001–2005)* throughout the United States—e.g., ACG Denver, Wisconsin, Philadelphia, Portland, Seattle, Kansas City, and Dallas—and

The Daily Deal (2001–2005) were first major business press to carry ACG news and advertorials on regular basis. Soon after came the relationship with Thomson Financial to co-brand a dealmakers' survey for ACG members and Thomson readers with results rolled out in individual press releases nationally and locally (launch: 2004).

Action (2): Building on excellent relationship with Thomson Financial and the ACG Dealmakers' Survey, the launch of a co-branded magazine, *ACG Mergers & Acquisitions Journal (MAJ)* in 2005, led by Mr. Hurley, solved a financial problem with *ACG Network*, provided improved thought leadership, and showcased the ACG brand before new, key audiences. The significant infusion of new revenue through advertising support enhanced ACG Global's financial reserve significantly.

STRENGTHENING CONNECTION
BETWEEN ACG GLOBAL AND ACG CHAPTERS

Chapter Leadership Meeting at InterGrowth

Direct communications among chapter leaders took a turn early in the twenty-first century, different than the 1990s, when ACG Global launched regional meetings for chapter leaders' give-and-take. The first ACG Chapter Leadership Meeting took place at InterGrowth in 2002, a result of the strategic planning completed a year before.

It was met with lukewarm interest, reflecting an underdeveloped format with "talking heads" populating the agenda.

As the program evolved—as soon as the following year—with the new chapter support team engaged, the meetings became all about sharing best practices in creative and systematic ways. Small chapters clustered with small chapters; larger with larger. The groups reshuffled based on geographic proximity and continued the exchange. A reshuffling again was based on member mix—corporate, service, private equity. Notes were recorded, discussed at the session, and shared throughout ACG in printed and e-mailed communications.

In 2004, as the event became more lengthy and robust, a seminar on how to conduct public relations was added. It was led by Bill Haynes, a board member employed by Magnet Communications. Enthusiasm for this type of addition (lecture by an authority) was apparent. Now the Chapter Leadership meeting had gained the momentum desired by board and staff years before. (*Brad Hughes, ACG Global chief operating officer in 2010, said that these meetings would continue in 2011 at InterGrowth as must-attend events, with discussion groups, speakers, and panels on a variety of subjects.*)

Other Meetings Have Legs, Carry Import

Regional Chapter Leadership meetings—first launched by ACG Global in the '90s in various regions of the country and designed for best practices exchange—were re-activated in 2007, according to Mr. Hughes. Different from the chapter leadership meeting held at InterGrowth, these gatherings were held "in the field." Regional meetings continue to advance communications and sharing of best practices, a contributing factor to the greater understanding and successful integration of ACG overall.

Corporate Issues Important in Denver

Clifford Pearl, ACG Denver's director of corporate member affairs, relayed an idea that sprouted from a regional meeting between ACG Denver and ACG Dallas. The discussion was attracting and retaining corporate membership (familiar ACG tune!). What developed was a "Corporate Plus membership" program to allure strategic members, according to Mr. Pearl, an attorney with Hensley Kim & Holzer, LLC.

"Denver does not have a large PEG community. Getting the corporate folks to participate is an ongoing struggle," said Mr. Pearl. The Corporate Plus program is an "affirmative outreach to Denver corporate potential members" that awards corporate-only benefits.

Additionally, the Chapters Administrators meeting, first held in June 2002 to provide a forum for best practices and information exchange, attracted a third of all administrators. It was a hit. Over the years, its attendance grew to include nearly 75 percent of administrators, and the venue, which began in the suburbs, moved to the city of Chicago at the request of attendees. The agenda changed to include volunteer leaders and staff leaders showcasing a skill or product and free-form roundtable discussions, much like the chapter leadership meetings at InterGrowth.

The administrators meeting was renamed the Chapter Executives meeting to in 2010 reflect the proper status of ACG administrative staffs who, as their chapters continued to grow, were taking on more executive activity and staffs of their own.

Note: The first recognition of the importance of the chapter administrator can be traced to the mid 1980s. By the mid-'90s, most chapters had administrative staffs, and by the twenty-first century, to our knowledge there are no chapters without these executives.

Private Equity Group (PEG) Marketplace Takes Off

The PEG Marketplace, first introduced as a two-hour showcase at InterGrowth in 2002 when Peter Coffey of Michael Best Fredrich LLP was chair, garnered the following description:

> *Check out the deal flow! A first-time event brought by popular demand: the Private Equity Group Marketplace gives equity groups and mezzanine funds an exclusive opportunity to display corporate materials and network with the many ACG dealmakers in attendance at InterGrowth® before enjoying a private cocktail reception for equity groups and mezzanine fund attendees only.*

Jeri Harman at InterGrowth Capital Connection early 2000's

A year later, the PEG Marketplace was opened to all attendees. The audience expanded to six hundred senior-level dealmakers who participated in a show that lasted three and a half hours.

According to ACG San Diego member Richard Haskel of The Delphos Group, the original concept for the PEG Marketplace came in the late 1990s from M&A Source, an organization of middle market intermediaries.

Jay Jester, of the Audax Group and veteran ACG leader, recalled it somewhat differently. He remembered when private equity groups became officially recognized in ACG.

"Charles [Conner], ACG Global president in 1998–1999, was one of the first to push adding private equity groups as a core membership division.

"Then in 2000, I remember sitting with ACG Boston members Ben Procter of Watermill Ventures and Stuart Mathews of Metapoint Partners. We were talking about how InterGrowth seemed like it was losing its appeal and was a bit tired. We floated the idea of adding an ACG Capital Connection, similar to one we'd launched in ACG Boston, to InterGrowth to make the event more appealing to PEGs and to mid-market investment banks. We planned the first ACG Capital Connection for the upcoming 2003 InterGrowth and were stunned that so many PEGs would pay $495 to buy a table. The first event oversold. It was a huge hit."

By 2005, there were eleven ACG Capital Connections conducted throughout ACG, and more than twenty similar events in 2006.

ACG InterGrowth Continues to Innovate

InterGrowth in 2005, chaired by Ardelle St.George of St.George & Carnegie, brought two new events to the conference: the ACG Virtual Trade Show, designed to foster the most productive use of time, and ACG Deal Source.

Ardelle St. George, ACG InterGrowth Chair 2005
at ACG InterGrowth-Palm Springs, CA

The Virtual Trade Show (VTS) greatly enhanced planning for a conference that was becoming more widespread and popular each year. The VTS encouraged registered attendees to visit acg.org before the conference to scroll through the attendee list and schedule one-off meetings in advance. The feature was also live to expedite meeting arrangements and deal-making opportunities on site.

ACG Deal Source, inspired by Patrick Hanratty of ACG Philadelphia, was described as "an all-new networking event at InterGrowth in 2005, providing the opportunity for investment bankers to meet privately with a variety of corporate and private equity groups in fifteen-minute sessions.

"Each banker who purchases a booth may host up to ten meetings arranged in advance through acg.org. Each booth is draped on three sides for a minimum of noise and visual interference," according to promotional material.

The event sold out the first year, the following year and the next. (Deal Source continues as an important business tool at InterGrowth in 2011.)

Deal Source meeting at ACG InterGrowth- Palm Springs, CA 2005

Branding Transforms View of ACG

Tucker Jump-Starts Process

Following the 2001 strategic plan issues related to ACG's image in the marketplace, Jim Tucker of Spectral Dynamics, Inc.—who would become ACG chairman a few years later—made the first move to find a branding firm. Mr. Tucker attended an ACG West Coast M&A Conference at which Clay Timon, chairman of Landor Associates, Inc., spoke on the power of brands. There, Mr. Tucker struck up a conversation with Landor's president of digital branding, Dave Studeman, suggesting "ACG could use some branding help." A few months later, Messrs. Studeman and Wangman met to set the wheels in motion.

Mr. Studeman communicated the value of branding in five bullet points that helped convince the ACG Global board:

1. *Support and strengthen all chapters*
2. *Drive membership and further improve quality of new members*
3. *Expand the organization by developing new chapters*
4. *Differentiate from competitive organizations, and*
5. *Unite the organization around a common vision while providing flexibility for chapters*

According to Mr. Studeman, "A critical aspect of this strategy was to revitalize the ACG brand and launch a campaign to build and strengthen ACG's internal and external worldwide image."

Charlie Downer, of then Downer & Co., became chairman of ACG in 2003 and rallied the branding troops.

Said Mr. Downer, "My presidency was mainly focused on a total rebranding for ACG, which consumed most of the board's effort during 2003 (and most of the bank account!). Since the beginning of ACG in the 1950s, the branding of the organization had slowly degenerated to the point where there were numerous logos, tag lines, color schemes, fonts, etc., being used by the chapters. By 2003, when I assumed the presidency, the problem had reached considerable proportions.

"This was a period of rapid expansion of the organization, with some of the larger chapters beginning to hold their own regional conferences, several of which were beginning to compete with InterGrowth in terms of size and importance. The brochures they produced were widely distributed and they added to the confusion in the marketplace of 'who' ACG was.

"Adding to the problem was the increasing use of the Internet with each chapter having its own website, often with their own logos, fonts, and tag lines that looked only vaguely like the 'official' version.

"Like most presidents of ACG," continued Mr. Downer, "my dialogue with Carl Wangman and members of the TCAG staff was frequent, and I relied on them for guidance and support. Carl and I agreed that the time to 'fix' the branding problem had arrived.

"Also very much involved in this decision was ACG Global board member Patrick Hurley, who was the vice president of marketing at the time."

Branding Firm Engaged

The board wrestled with several proposals from top branding firms and ultimately gave Dave Studeman, who left Landor and launched his own firm, Grey Ghost, Inc., about that time, and Magnet Communications the nod to steer. Mr. Hurley's leadership on the volunteer side provided key guidance of a large ACG branding committee charged with the oversight.

Said Mr. Downer, "Patrick did a superb job working with a blue-ribbon task force we assembled representing all the major constituencies in the association. He guided the consensus process on the multifaceted branding results from the 'promise,' to logo, color scheme, and tag line."

ACG InterGrowth Logo

At its rollout, the ACG brand statement, reflecting all key aspects, or pillars, upon which the organization stood, read as follows:

> *Founded in 1954, the Association for Corporate Growth (www.acg.org) is the premier global association for professionals involved in corporate growth, corporate development, and mergers and acquisitions for mid to large companies. Leaders in corporations, private equity, finance, and professional service firms focused on building value in their organizations belong to ACG. They recognize the multiple benefits of networking within an influential community of executives growing public and private companies worldwide. For fifty years, ACG members have focused on strategic activities that increase revenues, profits and, ultimately, stakeholder value.*

A much-desired "elevator pitch" came next. The succinct summary was easier to say "on the street." *"The benefits of our diverse membership, educational programs, access to industry leaders, expert insights, and unique culture make ACG the leading authority on corporate growth."*

Ultimately a tagline gained approval and popularity: *"ACG—the leading authority on corporate growth." In 2011, ACG changed the tagline to "Driving middle-market growth."*

Convincing members of the value of the new brand was less dramatic and more difficult, not the least part of which was explaining and handling cost factors. The branding process took nearly two years and exceeded budget significantly.

Mr. Downer said, "I don't think any of us realized how expensive the branding exercise was going to be. I received considerable criticism from members for having lavished too much on a useless exercise.

"In retrospect, I believe that the funds were well spent. With 12,000 members and nearly 50 chapters worldwide, a strong brand and identity provide an essential framework for a world-class professional association."

Mr. Downer is not alone in the positive assessment.

Paul Stewart, ACG Global chairman in 2007–2008, wrote a few years after his term, "The results [of branding] have been subtle on a year-to-year basis but very powerful over multiple years. For example, many today take for granted that names such as ACG Wisconsin, ACG Chicago, and ACG St. Louis seem logical, and that there is only one ACG 'green.' But before branding, multiple identities of ACG hindered the ability to build a foundation for national or global recognition of the organization," said the leader of PS Capital Partners, LLC, and adjunct professor at the University of Wisconsin Milwaukee.

Mr. Gullman added, "The branding issue has worked out well. I was skeptical about it. Too much money. I was absolutely wrong. Everyone knows what ACG is today."

More Strategic Planning Moves ACG to New Governance Structure, New Staff

Mr. Coffey's board during his chairmanship in 2005 undertook more strategic planning, this time facilitated by Ram Charan, an internationally recognized business consultant, speaker, and writer.

According to Messrs. Tucker and Stewart, the key recommendations from the multi-day planning session led to changes in board governance and the employment of a full-time staff executive with the title of president/CEO. The board hired Daniel Varroney, from the National Association of Manufacturers, to take on the position.

Jeri Harman of Allied Capital, a widely respected leader in ACG Los Angeles and ACG Global, chaired the task force in 2005 to reshape the governing structure of the organization, said Mr. Stewart.

Said Ms. Harman, "The change in corporate governance included a complete reworking of the bylaws and structure to provide a systematic inclusion of both large and small chapters in decision-making at the ACG Global level. It also included implementation of term limits ensuring 'fresh blood.' I chaired the ACG Corporate Governance committee, which drafted and put this into place."

Commented Mr. Stewart, "In hindsight, while it was hard to make the changes recommended by Mr. Charan, and the corporate governance committee work did not go as smoothly as planned, the end result was worth the organizational pain. The board governance changes were extensive and resulted in striking the proper balance of continuity, chapter representation, and rotation.

"And finding a CEO with the optimal experience and personality was not easy and required a second search a year later."

Dan Varonney, ACG Global CEO (2005-2007), ACG Global Chairman Patrick Hurley (2006-2007) and ACG Global Chairman Paul Stewart (2007-2008)

First Independent Office

Mr. Varroney set up ACG's first independent office in Palatine, Illinois. He focused on consolidating staff, buttressing revenue streams, developing public relations, but he struggled with internal systems management. He resigned his position in 2007 after two and a half years at the helm.

After an executive search, the second in three years, the ACG board employed Gary LaBranche, CEO of the Association Forum of Chicagoland for five years and chief executive for several other organizations prior. Mr. LaBranche took over ACG in September 2008. Within a few months, headquarters was moved to Chicago, key staff positions were added, and efforts were made to professionalize the Global staff operations.

But within a few short weeks after joining ACG, the worst economic downturn since the Great Depression impacted the country and the ACG community. While ACG membership dipped for only two months, InterGrowth attendance declined by 7 percent, and revenue from the *Merger and Acquisition Journal* fell dramatically. ACG management responded by tightening the budget and focusing on revenue-building opportunities. In the teeth of these struggles, ACG launched an extensive, long-planned new Internet platform to serve all chapters and members. This $500,000 project was seen as a long-term investment in ACG's future. "By adjusting to meet the challenges of the 'Great Recession,' and investing in new services and staffing, ACG is well-positioned to thrive over the next decade and beyond," said LaBranche.

"Now we can focus on the external environment and how we can create a better position for the capital community, particularly as we become more global, since capital is a cross-border commodity," said the CEO.

"ACG can use its significant strength to meet the increasingly difficult external environment and promote economic prosperity and job growth," he noted.

Mr. LaBranche's broad experience with associations is a clear advantage to ACG: he worked quickly with ACG's volunteer leaders to ascertain and develop opportunities created by the economic slump.

First-Time Public Policy Involvement

"ACG bylaws were changed in February 2010 to allow ACG to get involved in public policy issues," said Mr. LaBranche. "The global board arrived at this decision after very thoughtful analysis and dialogue. Through the efforts of the external relations committee, the board came to realize that ACG was the organization best positioned to tell the story of middle-market private capital. ACG's role going forward will not be focused on lobbying, but rather on education, research, and highlighting the job-creating, value-building role of private capital investment."

Mr. LaBranche summarized ACG today. "We are at a tipping point. Now ACG is a broader community and can build out from an internal to externally focused organization."

In 2011, ACG stands on solid financial footing with reserves of more than $2 million. InterGrowth 2011 achieved a record attendance of more than two thousand, with a net profit of $1.7 million. This level of attendance was nearly 15 percent of ACG's fourteen thousand members—a goal set by the board at the turn of the twenty-first century.

Gary LaBranche, ACG President and CEO (2008-Present)

Legal Needs Supported by Member with Long ACG History

ACG Global legal counsel Jim Easterling, who assumed the post in the early 1980s, offered commentary on the legal operations over the years. Much of his recollection covered issues that cropped up in the twenty-first century.

"Protecting ACG's intellectual property inside and outside the US came hand-in-hand with the branding process. Today the governing board is more selective about what to trademark and what not to protect legally."

Mr. Easterling noted two key legal requirements in recent years:

1. Incorporating the chapters separately for liability reasons and clarifying their roles and responsibilities. "We have

offered bylaws templates, generated paperwork necessary for incorporation, etc.," said Mr. Easterling, adding that the work began in 2005.

2. Revamping the governing structure and in 2006–2007, restructuring the board, giving chapters the majority vote. "This came about in response to the dissatisfaction with a dues increase, a measure passed by one vote during Jim Tucker's presidency," said Mr. Easterling. "There was a distinct feeling that the headquarters had grown apart from the chapters. This agreement (formalized in 2006 and 2007) spells out the role of ACG Global in serving the chapters."

Mr. Easterling's purview on ACG also tracks to earlier phenomena affecting its community.

Jim Easterling, ACG Global Legal Counsel (1980's-Present)

Private Equity Involvement Prompts Change

"The explosion of private equity and their enthusiasm for ACG led to the explosion in membership in the early 2000s," Easterling wrote. "ACG developed a separate membership category for them. Recently the membership has held at 12,000, quite an accomplishment."

Mr. Easterling answers definitively the question bandied about for the first thirty years of ACG: is ACG a luncheon club or a strong, centralized organization?

"One reason the membership has held despite the economy is the robust work of the chapters. They are stronger than luncheon clubs. Many chapters are very active organizations and supply value to members at rapid speed.

"The Chicago chapter focuses on energy, international events, and other niche interests that are cutting-edge," said the legal counsel of thirty years. "ACG chapters supply very high value and ACG Global has supplied the support to chapters who are offering the value."

On Growing Internationalism

Mr. Easterling commented on international maturity in ACG.

"ACG is on the cusp of international growth now. It's been a long time coming and required lots of support from the ACG staff to develop the international program. After a thriving chapter in the late 1990s and mid–2000s, there is no UK chapter today because new chapter leadership changed its membership criteria that don't fit ACG's model. The UK was looking for a high-end membership, serving corporate officers, and it doesn't fit with ACG's broader service, corporate, and PEG approach.

"ACG has chapter affiliation agreements with international hubs that lay out the same way as local chapters organize in the USA. Today there is more contact between ACG staff and international; staff members now provide direct service and support to ACG's eight non-North American chapters, and ACG leadership meets annually with leaders from these chapters. Now ACG has a chapter in China, the Czech Republic, and Spain, and is developing chapters in India and Brazil. 'Why this expansion?' asked Mr. Easterling, answering the query that has nagged ACG since its inception: Is ACG really an international organization or merely aspiring to be so?

"We have more members who do business internationally. The character of the US members has changed to focus on international business. The world has changed, and connecting internationally is becoming customary."

And in answer to current economic instability, Mr. Easterling points to ACG members' adaptability.

"Today the business climate has changed. Members are finding the private equity model built on acquisition, grow the portfolio companies and sell them at a profit does not work because financing is not available the way it once was. As a result, members are focusing on internal growth and effective management of the companies they have acquired. The deal is less important than managing the deals you have done.

"There is an enormous amount of talent in the marketplace that will come to the fore eventually. More financial regulation will not loosen credit but make it more difficult to come by," said Mr. Easterling.

Mid-Decade Strategic Planning Sharpens Direction Again

Bobby Blumenfeld, President ACG New York (2004-2010), Leslie Whittet, Vice President, ACG Chapter Operations, Harris Smith, (ACG Global Chairman (2008-2009), Craig Miller, CEO ACG Chicago

ACG Global governance continued in 2007 to focus on a limited number of multi-year initiatives to drive long-term value for ACG's members. A year-long strategic planning effort, facilitated by Jack

Derby, ACG Boston past chair and strategic planning professional with his own firm Derby Management, resulted in two new ACG initiatives: Global Expansion and the Essential Network. Global Expansion meant "expanding ACG's presence strategically in targeted markets while expanding elsewhere as opportunities arise."

Creating the Essential Network involved creating a digital platform to facilitate member networking, business sourcing, communication, and collaboration and enhanced chapter programming.

According to Ms. Whittet, ACG vice president of chapter operations, the launch of the refreshed ACG website with social networking hubs has made it easier for members to personalize the site, update their information, and find more in-depth information they need. *Note: In 1995 ACG launched into the Internet with a basic home page designed by American Eagle before it changed its name to americaneagle.com. Over the next fifteen years, americaneagle.com has played a vital role in the progression from that first simple post to the robust acg.org today.*

Mid-Decade Initiatives—Essential Network, Global Expansion, Global Growth Sponsorship, and Corporate Social Responsibility

Mr. Stewart echoed the value all strategic initiatives. "The board is attracting the top talent of ACG's membership and is providing strategic guidance and oversight of day-to-day operations. The Essential Network was launched, and ACG secured a presence in China, resurgence in Europe, and a chapter in India is on the horizon."

Harris Smith of Grant Thornton and ACG chairman 2008–2009, noted other global developments, such as a sponsorship program added in 2006. The Global Growth Sponsorship program is the highest level of ACG sponsorship anywhere within the organization. Dubbed a "partnership," it includes (as of this writing) four companies that partner with ACG for a period of time: Grant Thornton, Merrill, SAP, and most recently, Duane Morris.

Explained Mr. LaBranche, "As a global growth partner, Duane Morris shares its extensive intellectual capital and expertise on legal and regulatory issues. ACG members will benefit from this commitment, and Duane Morris will advance ACG's mission to drive middle market growth."

Harris Smith, ACG Global Chairman 2008-2009

Public Policy Movement Follows Backroom Service for Chapters

Den White, ACG chairman 2009–2010, said, "When I first joined the board, there was a growing belief that ACG Global needed to serve local chapters in new ways. We started streamlining and offering 'backroom' services for chapter events such as registration, better coordination with chapters to enhance their websites, etc.

"We refocused on growing internationally. In China, with Patrick Hurley's help, we became partners with the city of Tianjin. We first set up a non-profit entity in China with its own board of directors. This was not easy. We finally agreed to change our minds and set up a for-profit corporation; Hong Kong is the holding company with ACG Global as the parent. This is a first for-profit arm of ACG Global," added Mr. White, of McDermott, Will & Emory then and currently of Verrill Dana LLP.

Mr. White mentioned the public policy role alluded to first by Mr. LaBranche.

"The ACG Global board has given serious attention to the external challenges facing the middle-market growth capital and private equity community. Faced with these unprecedented challenges, we have taken unprecedented action. For the first time in its fifty-five-year history, ACG will be taking an active role in public policy dialogue. Our goal is to tell our story and ensure that the distinct voice of the mid-market is heard by federal policy makers and regulators."

Patrick Hurley, ACG Global Chairman 2006-2007 at ACG
InterGrowth 1995 (Speaking on China Initiative)

ACG Sponsored CIPEF Conference in Tianjin, China, June 9, 2008

As ACG Expands ...

... Chapter Staffing Needs Grow

A significant staffing change occurring in ACG—one that has occurred in at least three chapters—reflects the significance of ACG's growth and development. The hiring of full-time CEOs (or equivalent) with commensurate wages points to the challenges of managing especially large chapters today. Like managing the global office, managing Chicago, New York, and Los Angeles is more than full-time work. Craig Miller of ACG Chicago, Bobby Blumenfeld of ACG New York, and Bill Webster of ACG Los Angeles are the first to take on the expanded leadership roles.

Three of the founding chapters have moved out in front again.

... High-Profile Events Catch On Fast

Gary LaBranche noted, "There are exciting developments throughout ACG. The Los Angeles chapter deserves an enormous amount of credit for the ACG Cup. In 2010–2011, 30 chapters ran the Cup program, involving 115 graduate schools, 1,200 students, and $200,000 in scholarships and other awards.

"In addition, 85 percent of our chapters are involved in regional ACG Capital Connections. Chapters generate $15 million in gross revenues and net asset base or reserves are $9 million.

"ACG Global and its chapters today conduct more than 1,200 meetings with more than 50,000 attendees, pointing to the fact that the community served is much broader than the membership alone. There are stakeholders who follow ACG without joining the association."

... Member Needs Diversify More

Said Mr. White, "Job sourcing is another area of focus, even on the ACG website. Making ACG a job clearinghouse in the deal business is coming along. Employers and individuals have signed up for this benefit. ACG Global is uniquely positioned to add these elements to membership."

... Yet Some Things Remain the Same

Mr. Stewart summed up ACG's value beyond the numbers: "People make the difference. Over the years, at critical junctions, ACG was very fortunate to have committed people with the right blend of experience and personality for the task at hand. Some may call this luck or fate; I see it as a testimonial to the quality of the current and past administrative staff and members of ACG."

... 2011 Driving Middle-Market Growth

In January 2011, the ACG Global Board adopted a new strategic plan. Developed over a period of six months, the plan involved research from a member survey with more than 2,900 respondents. More than one hundred chapter leaders also provided input.

The resulting plan set a new mission, "Driving Middle-Market Growth," and established four key goals:

1. Enhance global presence to facilitate member business relationships—**Local Community, Global Reach**
2. Serve diverse member needs via useful products and services—**Diverse Needs, Targeted Services**
3. Facilitate business connections via technology—**Access Anytime, Business Anywhere**
4. Provide strong a voice for middle market private investment— **Private Investment, Public Good**

This plan is expected to lead ACG's efforts through the year 2015.

CHAPTER 5

ACG New York

1950s–1970s
PETER HILTON, CRUSADER

Peter Hilton of the Corporate Diversification Corp. was the visionary. He was the dealmaker who saw the potential of ACG in the 1950s. From the start, luncheons at the Plaza Hotel and the like brought them together—he and other middle-market investment bankers and corporate dealmakers, who built friendships and business and expounded on ideas.

Some of the more luminescent attendees in the earliest days, according to Don Reed, who went on to become an ACG Global president in 1976, included business leaders Murray Sanders of Martin Marietta, Clifford Woods of First National City Bank (Citibank), Tony Haas of General Foods (ACG Global President 1975–1976), Neil Bandler, Steve Helpern of Arthur Anderson (ACG Global president 1981–1982), John May, William E. Hill, Carl Hagelin (ACG Global president 1978–1979) of Marshall & Stevens.

An early ACG advocate, Mr. Reed recalled, "In the early '60s, I began attending the New York luncheons when possible from Ohio and was present when we formally formed ACG. Peter Hilton was the driving force, although well supported by some of the original luncheon group."

Mr. Reed told a sad, important story. "Peter Hilton died in 1974. Being somewhat of a gardener, our distinguished founder was trimming a hedge around his home in lower Connecticut, I seem to recall, when his electric trimmers hit a bees' nest, resulting in his being bitten badly. He was hospitalized and lingered painfully in the aftermath with his health damaged. Impaired, he attended one more InterGrowth in Phoenix and died soon afterward."

The following year, in 1975, members created the Peter Hilton Award to honor the founder. They presented it, appropriately, to a company of high standards, The Franklin Mint. Founded in 1964 when it began striking legal-tender coins for foreign countries' commemorative medallions, casino tokens, and precious-metal ingots, The Franklin Mint built its reputation on "an uncompromising commitment to excellence, attention to detail, and a vibrant spirit of innovation that continues to set industry standards," according to the company website.

Mr. Reed noted that two years later, when he was immediate past president, "I had the honor of presenting the award to the chairman of Halliburton Company, John Harbin.

"I presume it is still being awarded," he said.

Other New York Leaders Rule ACG

Gary Fiebert, who was with Gilbert Tweed Associates, Inc., served as president of the New York chapter in 1980 and became ACG Global president just two years later.

Hunt Whitacre of RJR Nabisco (ACG Global president 1987–88) joined ACG New York in the early '80s because he "knew that mergers and acquisitions would be important to [his] business. ACG filled a need by educating people about corporate growth at all levels," he said, adding that ACG's niche was carved, and the middle market prevailed. "Large investment bankers were not members."

Mr. Whitacre recalled that ACG Global would often select for InterGrowth speakers business leaders who had addressed ACG New York meetings. Examples were Brian Little of Forstmann Little, a major equity firm, who was also interested in the triathlon; and Mike Milligan of Drexel, "a very passionate person with fire in his eyes."

He added, "When I was New York program chair, we sought out speakers that would allow us to see behind the resumes."

It was Mr. Whitacre's involvement with Financial Executives Institute (FEI) *(which became Financial Executives International in 2001)* that gave birth to the first ACG Global publication, the *Journal for Corporate Growth*. Its high-gloss finish and in-depth stories reflected the kind of panache he wished for ACG. Mr. Whitacre also discussed working on the *Journal* with Margaret Glos, owner of the management firm responsible for managing ACG New York at the time. He spoke highly of Paul Gaddis, who eventually was hired as editor from 1988 to 1993, the year it was discontinued.

Late 1980s and '90s:
New Ideas, Leaders Impact Member Rolls

Said Alan Gelband, who joined ACG New York in 1987, "I was immediately recruited to be assistant treasurer of the chapter.

"At that time, there was a policy of offering free lunches to prospects. The chapter had about 400 members [actual number: 410], and I would bring as many as six guests to the luncheons. Many joined.

"Nobody wanted to be president, so I took the job. We continued to grow. By the end of 1988, we had nearly 450 members."

Mr. Gelband, of his own firm, Alan Gelband Co., continued, "My approach was to find rock-star speakers who had really accomplished something, as opposed to those who only offered theories about business. I remember vividly that on September 15, 1988, Tom Lee [Thomas H. Lee Company] spoke about the Playtex deal [where the Lee company was the major investor in a $1.3 billion buyout]."

Sam Zell, Merrill Halperin, chairman of Charter Group, Jerry Levin, CEO or Revlon, Jay Jordan, general partner of Jordan's Private Equity firm, Ted Forstmann of Forstmann Little in the midst of the RJR Nabisco "so-called fiasco" were some of the speakers who addressed the chapter during Mr. Gelband's presidency.

Mr. Gelband, called by his peers, "a charismatic networker," continued to make moves to promote the chapter and attract members. He was among a fistful of advocates of the "black-tie dinner" first held at the Waldorf Astoria with an attendee gathering of about one hundred ACG members and guests.

Mr. Gelband recalled the creation of a small scholarship fund with recipients from NYU and Fordham University, yet lamented "the chapter ebbed and flowed often, as did the financial business at the time."

He continued to recruit members, and one talented colleague/friend in particular helped him out. Burt Alimansky, chairman of Alimansky Capital Group and founder of the New York Capital Roundtable, was just finishing a term as president of the Harvard Business Club.

"I'd had lots of experience in managing this kind of organization [like ACG], so I did get involved," said Mr. Alimansky. "The first thing I did was put together a business plan with things on it like, Who do you want to recruit to be involved, how and when?

"I wanted people who joined to satisfy their own best interests," he said. "People who wanted visibility to help grow their businesses."

Employing Systems Builds Membership

But membership was a struggle, he recalled. "It had to do with having a systematic way to attract and keep members. We had to become 'network conscious' and pay attention to the details."

Mr. Alimansky talked about the importance of "back-office" assistance. The first one, he recalled, was his office at The Capital Roundtable. "We handled meeting details, not membership rolls, which were taken on by the headquarters in Chicago."

Managing the chapter also had to do with strategy and standardizing the program, said Mr. Alimansky. "When I was there, it was a scramble to get a speaker. It was the same song: let's get 'so-and-so-big-wig' to speak. Lots of people in New York didn't care about the big-name speakers because they were concerned with bigger deals than ACG members did.

"So I insisted on panels, like 'Raising Debt in 1991,' and it didn't really matter who you got to speak, so long as he or she was reasonably sane. The topic was more important."

Advance planning, early communication, and a tailored approach were also key. Mr. Alimansky would deliberately add an educational program like "Deal Structure" or "Best Practices for Managing an Investment Banking Boutique" to appeal to a select group of members, rather than the whole.

Contending with Local Membership Issues

Mr. Alimansky articulated the particular conundrum of ACG New York. Its membership, heavily filled with investment banking firms and other financiers, did not match the Midwestern ACG pattern that attempted to balance service and corporate firms.

At one point, Mr. Alimansky told his friend Phil Nielsen in ACG Chicago, "Phil, you need to understand the difference in New York. Coopers & Lybrand, Goldman Sachs are corporate partners here. They are not service providers. New York really is different from the rest of the country. There is not a whole lot of manufacturing, as there is in the Midwest. New York is a world unto itself."

During Mr. Alimansky's regime, ACG black-tie dinners became bigger and more star-studded. John Whitehead, former US Undersecretary of State and chairman of Goldman Sachs, attended an ACG New York event at the United Nations. "It was a big money-maker," said Mr. Alimansky. "With these events, we began to have a bank account. I believed, let's spend it and the people will pay for it, and they did."

Mr. Alimansky says that through the years, ACG continues to be about networking, deal-making, and market intelligence.

"Essentially ACG is about people in middle-market deal-making and middle-market finance getting together to do business. It still offers incalculable value to people's careers and organizations, in ways that senior executives of large organizations would not relate to.

"ACG is not about Goldman [Sachs] or Blackstone. Its networking orientation has made it vital to the private equity firms. They are not ACG, but they depend upon ACG.

"It is not a private equity organization, but there is a wonderful symbiosis. ACG needs the revenue that the PEGs bring in. But when you go to the lunches in New York, the PEGs are not there.

"In a funny way, ACG hasn't changed over the years," said Mr. Alimansky. "It's for the smaller, middle-market kind of business lender, investment banker, just as it was fifty years ago."

57 Varieties—ACG New York Style in the Twenty-first Century

A flurry of activity and diversity early in the twenty-first century took ACG New York to a new level of impact. The ambitious schedule plugging targeted interests *(some fifty-seven programs in 2011, according to chapter executive Lou Halstead)* revealed the chapter's prodigious growth and audience reach. ACG New York President Bobby Blumenfeld, now executive director of the chapter, filled in the blanks for the most recent decade.

Bobby Blumenfeld, President ACG New York
(2004-2010) and Executive Director (2010-Present)

Private Equity Directs

"If I had to pick a time that the chapter started to reverse course and begin its evolutionary growth," said Mr. Blumenfeld, "it would be in 2002, when we started to focus on private equity firms and other capital providers. I remember Jay Jester of Audax [ACG Boston], who assisted our chapter in putting together our first Capital Wine Connection in 2003. In addition, I realized that even though we were growing the chapter by 10 to 15 percent a year, it would take a greater effort to grow the chapter more and spread our message more widely.

"As my background is in both restructuring and turning around businesses, I excel at promoting business revenues and controlling expenses. My concept that the chapter adopted was to begin moving away from lunch programs, create new types of events, vary locations, and promote our efforts.

"In 2003, Calvin Navatto at Sun National Bank was appointed president, and I was appointed president-elect," said Mr. Blumenfeld.

"Over the course of the last seven years, the chapter has seen an evolutionary increase in membership, reserves (our reserves have grown by approximately 500 percent since 2005), attendance [in 2005, 2,350 attendees, to 7,000+ projected in year 2011], programming, and recognition in the New York financial world."

New and sustaining programs hosted over the decade include:

ACG Capital Connection Wine Event launched in 2003

Our most well-known event began at the suggestion of Mr. Jay Jester, with the first event at the New York Athletic Club.

Tri-State Conference launched in 2004

This unites the New York, New Jersey, and Connecticut chapters in a joint program, which was renamed the "Tri-State Green Conference" in 2010.

ACG Tri-State Conference 2004-Mark Kuehn (President ACG New Jersey), Bobby Blumenfeld (President ACG New York) and Kevin Fiala (President ACG Connecticut)

ACG Stratton Ski Networking Conference (New York and Boston) launched in 2006

Now in its fifth year, this conference, which in its first year saw 18 attendees, has attracted in some years 130 participants and averages around 90. It has a reputation as one of the best networking events offered. The event began after Mr. Blumenfeld and Jack Derby (ACG Boston chairman) came up with the idea to hold the event at the Stratton Mountain Club, one of the most prestigious ski-club buildings in America.

ACG New York and Boston Ski Conference 2007 at Stratton Mountain, Vermont

WinterBash/Monte Carlo Networking Night launched in 2005

Typically held in January, the event has been held in the Roosevelt Hotel, Tavern on the Green, Sky Club, and the Mid-Town Executive Club. More than 150 attend this popular event. In the past, ACG New York has donated a free trip to Monte Carlo and other points in Europe. An awards component was tried in 2008 but soon afterward was abandoned. This event was changed to WinterBash in 2011.

M&A DealSource—the Beer Event launched in 2005

To complement the event for private equity firms (serving wine), we decided upon a different event that catered to investment bankers and invited private equity firms to meet sources of deal flow.

ACG New York-Sponsored InterGrowth Party launched in 2003

ACG New York sends more of its members to InterGrowth than any other chapter. It has done so for decades. With this in mind, ACG New York has sponsored a theme party over the last five years at InterGrowth to provide value to its members as well as increase the visibility of the chapter. Themes have included: disco, the Blues Brothers, the Grateful Dead, Li'l Nathan-Louisiana music, and Jeff McBride's Magic Show, Jimmy Buffet, and the Paperback Writers featuring the Beach Boys and Beatles.

ACG New York party at ACG Intergrowth 2006
(Orlando, Florida) featuring the Alabama Blues Brothers

Golf Event launched in 2005

Under the direction of Jeffrey Wurst (Ruskin Moscou Faltischek, P.C.), this event attracts upwards of one hundred golfers to network on the links. For the last few years, it has been held at the Agawam Golf Club in Rye.

ACG/TMA Distressed Conference launched in 2007

When we first held this conference, the economy was strong, and many members didn't understand our motivation. However, by the second conference, its importance became all too apparent as the financial markets began to melt in the summer and fall of 2008. This event also marked the beginning of co-venturing with complementary financial associations.

Senior Lenders Panel launched in 2006

Held in May, this panel is a forum for our members to hear from the top leveraged and asset-based lenders in New York and throughout the United States.

SummerBash launched in 2004

Held in June, the SummerBash marks the end of the second quarter. SummerBash was originally led by David Soloway of The Madison Group.

Asian Market Program launched in 2005

This conference has focused primarily on China.

Corporate Investor Panel launched in 2008

Originally led by David Deutsch of DND & Co., this October program features investment banking, private equity, and corporations discussing issues of the day. It is now known as the State of the Capital Markets, led by Blake Hornick of Seyfarth Shaw.

Emerging Professionals Night launched in 2007

To attract the next level of aspiring financial professionals, this event introduces ACG to a group that usually needs and wants to sharpen their networking skills.

Health Care Conference launched in 2009

Now in its fourth year, the Health Care Conference was an idea of Bill Kane (Red Born Capital), Steve Goldsmith (HFG), and others to assemble a specialty conference for those interested in investments in the health care sector. It attracts some four hundred attendees.

Educational Cup launched in 2009

Led by Carlos Ferreira (Grant Thornton) and begun in 2009, ACG New York sponsors a competition among area MBA financial students from Cornell, NYU, Fordham, Pace, Hofstra, and Baruch.

ACG New York Expansion: Westchester and Long Island Divisions

We have successfully launched programs in the suburbs to attract more corporate members and financial firms.

Chaired by Lee Justo of Neczus, Westchester programming launched in 2007 has included scotch tasting, logistics and distribution, ACG Capital Connection, and fine dinners that have been held in locations including the Westchester Country Club, the Four Seasons, and X20.

Chaired by Barry Garfield of Holtz Rubenstein Reminick, Long Island Programming began in 2009 with our first program in the summer featuring Jerry Buccino, chairman of Buccino & Associates. Attendance: +150.

ACG New York and Utah Ski Event launched in 2009

The idea was to collaborate with other chapters and interest ACG New York members (especially those who like to ski) in an event that features "champagne snow." Our first event was held at the Canyons in 2009 (netting a joint profit of $11,000 used to support subsequent ski events), the second in Park City and the third back at the Canyons. In 2011, the Los Angeles and San Francisco chapters also provided their support. ACG Utah holds its ACG Capital Connection in conjunction with this event.

Ex-Presidents Committee

In order to preserve the history and direction of ACG New York, the chapter has valued the input of its former leadership. Current active members include: Messrs. Alimansky, Gelband (former ACG New York and ACG Global president), David Cunn, and Mr. Navatto.

ACG New York Champions Awards, launched in 2011

Held at Sotheby's Auction House, this new program honored the top leading nominated middle market deals and firms in the New York market. Bobby Blumenfeld, former President of ACG New York and current executive director, was presented with the Peter Hilton Award for his past services.

Leadership change at ACG New York in 2010

In 2004 Mr. Blumenfeld became ACG New York President. Under his leadership the chapter grew to more than 900 members and increased its event offerings to more than 50 events annually in three locations, Manhattan, Westchester and Long Island. Given the amount of growth experienced by the chapter, the ACG New York Board voted in early 2010 to create a full-time executive director position and offered it to Mr. Blumenfeld, who was pleased to accept. Upon Mr. Blumenfeld's resignation as president, the board nominated Stephen V. Prostor, director of Financial Sponsors Lending at The Citigroup PrivateBank, to assume the position. He was re-elected president in January 2011.

Mr. Prostor had joined ACG New York in 1997 after relocating from Texas. At the time, the chapter had about 200 members and annually hosted ten to twelve events, which were primarily luncheons with speakers. Initially his membership helped Mr. Prostor build and establish a network of contacts in the New York area. Over time, he became more involved as a committee member, committee chair, board member, executive committee member, and eventually president.

Under Mr. Prostor's leadership ACG New York took additional steps to "raise the bar" on the chapter's value proposition by adopting a three-year strategic plan and a conflict-of-interest policy; establishing a communications committee and a non-profit foundation, "ACG Cares New York Chapter;" and entering into long-term employment agreements with Mr. Blumenfeld and Chapter Executive Lou Halstead. ACG New York was recognized as 2010 Chapter of the Year at ACG InterGrowth in 2011.

That is just for starters as we move into the second decade of the twenty-first century!

ACG New York makes a $5,000 donation to
the Robin Hood Foundation 2008

Steve Prostor, ACG New York President (2010-)
and ACG Global Board Member

CHAPTER 6

ACG Chicago

ACG Chicago Forms Hub in 1968, Spawns Leaders and Invention

Donald Reed explained that he became interested in starting a chapter after discovering the value of the ACG New York chapter. But he needed something closer to work.

"After doing several acquisitions as chief engineer at Aro Corp. in Bryan, Ohio, in 1964, I moved to Chicago to become senior vice president of acquisitions at National Can Corp. and then took a more serious interest in ACG New York meetings," said Mr. Reed.

The distance between work and chapter became burdensome, said the man who with National Can had "some forty acquisitions" and in 1967 set up the Donald G. Reed Corp. in Chicago.

"So I became quite involved in the formation of a Chicago chapter, the first chapter outside of New York, in 1968." His one-year presidency started immediately.

Booz, Allen & Hamilton acquired his firm in 1969 and called it Booz Allen Acquisition Services, Inc., with offices in Chicago, New York, and later London. Mr. Reed was president.

"The Chicago chapter of ACG grew quickly, with early leaders including Fred Roberton, Tom Smith, James Ryan, Hugh Wagner, Ken Bony, Bill Howell, John Holmes, and many others whom Tom, Fred, and I recruited," relayed Mr. Reed.

In 1972, Fred Roberton, supported by others, expressed the need for all of the chapters to have an annual get-together, which they called InterGrowth. Mr. Reed recalled that the Chicago chapter led in the organization of the first InterGrowth meeting in 1972 in Mexico City, "with solid support from Peter Hilton and others in the New York chapter.

"Attendance at the Mexico City meeting came in around fifty couples, including some notables like the American Ambassador to Mexico, Bob McBride, and Don Rumsfeld, who was then counselor to President Richard Nixon. I well remember a private tour of the embassy for several of us. It was a very successful start for InterGrowth.

"When InterGrowth was being organized, we decided that if it succeeded in Mexico City, we would meet annually at very nice sites, alternating each year from the East Coast to the West Coast, interspersed with occasional foreign meetings."

Keeping Membership "Balance"

"All chapters were growing well as the organization became more widely known," said Mr. Reed. "Our heavy membership of corporate officers and management seemed to be an incentive for the services [accounting, lawyers, banking, consultants, etc.] to become interested in ACG, and I recall board meeting discussions about how to achieve a more balanced membership."

Commented Warner Rosenthal, who also became involved with ACG in 1969, "I attended the first ACG meeting at the Ambassador East Hotel in 1969 when I was vice president of corporate development for E.R. Moore Co., a division of Beatrice Foods Co. Don Reed from Chicago was in charge, and Peter Hilton from New York led the discussion. It was a short meeting at the end of a workday, with punch and cookies and visiting and networking. The meeting was for Peter to tell the Chicago group that ACG is important.

"I recall a focus on corporate members, but service people were the ones who wanted to meet," added Mr. Rosenthal.

A few years later, Mr. Rosenthal went into business for himself and let his ACG membership lapse. He would rejoin later and become part of the Global board in 2000.

"I rejoined when a lady from RR Donnelley asked me to attend an ACG Chicago meeting."

Mr. Rosenthal took over the awards area for the chapter when the Peter Hilton Award was created in 1975. He continued as ACG Chicago's award chair for five years. "A few of our nominees advanced to InterGrowth," said the man, who remains enthusiastic about the depth and intent of the program.

ACG Chicago Leaders Move Up the Chairs

Gebelein, Rosenthal, Tucker, Others ...

In 2000, Chris Gebelein of Borg-Warner & Co. in Chicago and president of ACG Global, brought Mr. Rosenthal onto the ACG board, where he served as secretary and treasurer. Mr. Rosenthal in turn brought George Stevenson of Stevenson & Co. to the ACG Global board. Mr. Stevenson had been president of ACG Chicago.

During the four years that Mr. Rosenthal served at the global level, he and the leadership team started to focus on "buyout groups, who were the bridge between service and corporate development officers," said Mr. Rosenthal.

"Buyout managers wanted to meet the service providers, and they came in with corporate subsidiaries. They were aggressive. They were everything we wanted in ACG. I pushed and others pushed [for their greater involvement]. I felt it was important to increase our credibility and to become a more significant organization.

"ACG was not as prestigious then as it was to become. Now representatives of industry are members; they were outsiders then."

Jim Tucker of Spectral Dynamics, Inc., also came to ACG Chicago early. It was the first of several chapters he would join.

"I joined ACG Chicago in the mid-'70s at the request of Tom Smith, the first president and eventual honorary director. Tom had arranged the deal for the first company I purchased, which was in Cincinnati. It made a long commute to meetings.

"Subsequently, I moved to Southern California, where I became a member of ACG Los Angeles and a board member in the '80s," added Mr. Tucker, whose affiliation today rests with ACG Orange County.

... Easterling, Nielsen, Stokely, Rice

In 1981, Jim Easterling of Ungaretti & Harris in Chicago became legal counsel for ACG Global. He joined ACG through the encouragement of his partner, Steve Slavin, who was also a member. As legal counsel during the presidency of Steve Halpern, Mr. Easterling said the first issues "that continue today were making sure ACG and its chapters secured tax-exempt status and protecting ACG's intellectual property.

"Since Mr. Halpern was in Chicago, we moved the legal office to

Chicago from New York City," said Mr. Easterling. (*Note: A young professional woman, Maria DiCara, became the administrator of ACG Chicago. Ms. DiCara was the connection to the Lurie-Murphy Company, which managed ACG Global during the '80s, surmised Mr. Easterling.*)

Phil Nielsen, another eventual president of ACG Global, lived in Paris until the mid-'70s. When he returned to Chicago, he became the A.C. Nielsen vice president of international business opportunities—developing new services for Nielsen, finding new products, generating new ideas.

"A.C. Nielsen was not acquisitive. It was focused on internal growth, service product line expansion, broadening customer base, marketing," said Mr. Nielsen. A Los Angeles contact persuaded Mr. Nielsen to go to InterGrowth in 1978 at the Arizona Biltmore. There he realized ACG members might help him find new business prospects for A.C. Nielsen and became active in the organization, eventually becoming ACG Global president in 1989.

Mr. Nielsen found surveys—for which the company is renowned—were difficult at ACG because they concerned M&A activity and deals made through ACG. "It was tough to decide who was involved in the deal and to discern if multiple respondents were reporting on the same deal and skewing the numbers."

Craig Stokely of The Stokely Partnership, who quickly became an active member of the Chicago chapter starting in 1986, served on the Chicago chapter board. Among several comments, Mr. Stokely said, "It was a pleasure to also meet and work with Tom Smith, one of the 'fathers of ACG.'"

Mr. Stokely's firm was selected to lead the 2001 strategic planning process for ACG Global, which took place in Chicago during Russ Robb's presidency. The plan laid the groundwork for important activity to come, including governance changes and branding.

Strength for International Charge

Longtime ACG member and advocate Andy Rice started with ACG Chicago in the late 1980s. "I joined ACG Chicago in 1988 while working for Ameritech. Then I joined Jordan Industries and The Jordan Company in 1989 and continued to stay active."

Mr. Rice held ACG Chicago offices of vice president of membership and programs before he became the first chairman of the international committee, which immediately became a vibrant arm of the chapter. The international committee to this day sponsors regular events and publishes a quarterly newsletter. It has held, over the recent years, three major one- or two-day conferences attended by two hundred to three hundred participants.

"I have also spoken at numerous ACG chapter events on doing deals and expanding into China, India, and Brazil," said Mr. Rice.

Like many engaged ACG Chicago members, Mr. Rice became active with ACG globally before too long. "I served on the ACG Global board in the late 1990s and am currently serving on it again [as of this writing] as chairman 2011–2012. I am active with our efforts to expand ACG overseas."

In addition to communications advances like the Internet and mobile phone expansion worldwide, Mr. Rice credits "many ACG relationships worldwide that have helped The Jordan Company in the US and internationally.

"Over the past twenty years, more than half of all our company's deals involved someone from ACG, either the broker/intermediary that introduced the deal to us or a lawyer or accountant representing the seller. The relationships we have nurtured through ACG have helped us find and get deals done.

"The relationships have come from ACG Chicago and globally at ACG InterGrowth," said the member, who has served on the InterGrowth committee seven times and has spoken at InterGrowth four times on China, Central Europe, and other international topics.

"I have enjoyed playing tennis at InterGrowth and have found it a great way to network with other members from around the US and overseas. I met Harald Klien of CDI Beteiligungsberatung based in Vienna playing tennis at InterGrowth. Several years later, one of my colleagues, Torben Luth, sponsored several ACG events in Vienna with Harald Klien, which led to the formation of the chapter there." *(Mr. Klien, who continues to serve on the chapter and global levels of ACG, is a longtime InterGrowth attendee and ACG proponent.)*

More recently, Mr. Rice, who represents the company that became one of the first InterGrowth sponsors—"The Jordan Opening

Reception," as it was dubbed in the early '90s—was involved in setting up the China chapter.

"My colleague, Youming Ye, helped organize and host the exploratory chapter meetings in Beijing and Shanghai, which led to the formation of ACG China. The ACG Global board appointed Mr. Ye the first chairman of ACG China."

Close-Knit Chapter Tries New Venues

The Chicago chapter had three hundred members in 1991, so that "closer personal relationships with all of the members were possible," said Mr. Stevenson. "Chicago had activities that were primarily monthly meetings with a variety of informative speakers and one or two social events per year. At the time, the economy was in a downturn, so our goal was to maintain and increase membership and improve services to our members.

"But," said Mr. Stevenson, "Chicago was always a strong chapter for attendance at InterGrowth. We informally would vie with New York for the greatest attendance each year."

The Chicago chapter, in its twenty-fifth year, was the third largest, trailing New York and Boston. In 1995, it relaxed its structure and added a suburban breakfast meeting to its monthly city-based luncheon program.

"We did this principally to accommodate the increasingly far-flung membership," according to Mr. Stevenson.

The chapter continued its support of InterGrowth, which was led in 1993 by Chicago member and business entrepreneur Patricia Buus, who conceived of the innovative Deal Mart and Breakfast Roundtables programming.

Diversity Leads the Way

Craig Miller, CEO of ACG Chicago since 2006, joined the ACG Chicago board of directors in the mid-'90s "when programming needed help." His focus was to increase the quantity and quality of chapter activities.

"In 2000 or 2001, we started strategic planning in Chicago," said Mr. Miller. "It was a critical factor in successful programming for the chapter, which started to build a plan around growing in influence with less regard for quantity."

In 2006, Mr. Miller became the chapter's first CEO, a paid office. One of his first strategic decisions was to develop a business model he called the "four vertical silos of membership, which include: 1-Corporate; 2 - International; 3 - M&A/Private Equity; and 4 - Venture/ New Economic Growth.

Mr. Miller's motto became "ACG Chicago—getting bigger by getting smaller."

"At the end of the day, we are always looking at adding member value. Where is the member going to pick up the next value? This kind of thinking directs the programming for ACG Chicago.

"Each of the vertical silos does strategic planning. For example, the international network is refining its approach, offering simple, smaller programs rather than huge events. For instance, the Turkish ambassador visited and spoke in 2009 to just thirty people. And that's okay.

"The great variety of programming *[ACG Chicago offers more than thirty-five programs a year, about three a month including a Midwest ACG Capital Connection]* serves the interests of each member silo. This strategically based plan has worked well. Chicago is now the largest chapter with more than a thousand members, one hundred serving on committees and fifty leading the four verticals."

Technology Builds Member Ties

The silo strategy vis-à-vis ACG global has import, according to Mr. Miller, who describes ACG chapters as clients to ACG Global. The core mission is "serving chapters and members."

He describes ACG as "a tribal nation," explaining, "what works in Chicago doesn't necessarily work in other places. One of the great benefits of ACG's global technology is its ability to serve the different demographics of each chapter, bringing them close but also letting them be themselves. The best-practice calls still in play are critical to letting chapters grow their own way."

Mr. Miller chaired the mid-twenty-first initiative called the *Essential Network,* a technology program developed with ACG Global and americaneagle.com that operates as ACG's proprietary social network. Its goal is connectivity, connecting members with similar interests.

Handling the project involved "creating a digital platform to facilitate member networking, business sourcing, communication, collaboration, and enhanced chapter programming," he added.

On Collaborative Programming

After rejecting requests from some organizations, ACG Chicago has looked favorably on working cooperatively with other relevant groups— the Chicagoland Chamber of Commerce, the Council on Global Affairs, Northwestern University's Kellogg School of Management, and others. The collaboration with respected groups like these has made for "great programming," remarked the CEO.

On Corporate Programming

Mr. Miller is mindful of all kinds of ACG members. He noted that ACG Chicago has 130 corporate development members and "expects to double it in the next few years" through programs pointedly corporate. He mentioned a few:

- An author series on relevant topics
- Roundtables with twenty to thirty corporate development officers discussing corporate development issues at dinners and breakfasts staged on Chicago's west and north sides
- The clean-tech side of venture in its fourth year of programming
- Diversity-side of communities (last year had two hundred people in attendance and in later years expect to draw on census patterns to relook at diversity—not just in the M&A field, but in the workplace as well)
- China program ("drew two hundred attendees")

On Social Responsibility

Corporate Social Responsibility is defined by ACG as "an extended commitment made by an executive or business to produce a clear and explicitly positive impact on society. A company can make this positive impact simply by acting in an ethical manner and contributing to economic development while encouraging community growth and advancement."

Executives who are committed to giving back contribute not only money but time and expertise at charitable organizations that would not otherwise have the resources to serve the community.

The ACG Chicago members are proud to provide assistance to various Chicago, regional, and national charitable organizations. "It is our hope that by supporting such a diverse variety of organizations, we are contributing to the overall improvement of our community," said Mr. Miller.

As of this writing, forty-five charities and twenty-six members are noted in this initiative on the ACG Chicago website.

On Relationships

Mr. Miller, like many ACG leaders since its inception, places a high value on the relationships formed through ACG. ACG Chicago has developed a member approval process that ensures a senior-level, quality membership that makes the chapter network meaningful and "keeps retention high," according to Mr. Miller. "This adds to trust and strengthens the sense of community.

"You cannot take the community and personal aspect away from ACG, regardless of how sophisticated the technology. Electronics are designed for communication and outreach, but ACG is successful because it hasn't forgotten the importance of community and trust with members."

CHAPTER 7

ACG Toronto

1971
FIRST INTERNATIONAL FOOTPRINT

The leadership of the New York and Chicago chapters envisioned the scope of the organization beyond the United States and looked to Toronto as a logical international site for a chapter.

There was a clear reason to choose Toronto. Tom Smith, one of the organizers of the Chicago chapter, was a partner at Ernst & Ernst (in 1989 to become Ernst & Young). He knew Robert Coffey was doing international work in Toronto, and "the Coach," as Mr. Coffey is known, was working with Ernst & Ernst at the time. Coach was a go-getter.

Mr. Coffey became the driving force behind the Toronto chapter. He attended the first InterGrowth in Mexico City (another evidence of the "international tone" of the early days.) The Coach described efforts to start the chapter in 1971.

"I got together a group of about ten people. These were high-profile businessmen, most from the service side, about 30 percent from the corporate side. People like senior partners of Richardson Securities, which was owned by the Richardson family, one of Canada's most distinguished families. It also owned 8 percent of Canadian Imperial Bank of Commerce (CIBC). We tried to get folks who could make an impact—security dealers, lawyers, and corporate people."

Peter Hilton, ACG founder, attended the first ACG Toronto meeting. He talked about corporate growth with emphasis on internal growth or negative acquisitions—divesting a business to allow for core company growth. Warren Avis, founder of the eponymous rental-car company, spoke at the second chapter meeting. Duff Roblin, fourteenth premier of Manitoba from 1958–1967, was another key speaker in the early days.

ACG Podium Logo

Leaders Emit Rally Cry

The first meeting of ACG Toronto attracted 125 people, said Mr. Coffey. The presidents of Ford, GM, and Chrysler called upon the Toronto Dominion Bank (TDB), and asked it to forward invitations to key clients.

According to Coach Coffey, "TDB helped us a great deal in those early years. The bank could see value in ACG. In fact, the bank gave each guest speaker an original soapstone carving from the bank's collection. We paid a very low price for such a rare memento."

Eighty people attended the second meeting, which was operating "on a shoestring," according to the Coach.

In 1975, he became the fourth InterGrowth chair. The Bermuda meeting was the last conference to be held offshore. Victor Korn of the worldwide executive recruiting Korn/Ferry firm and "Buzz" McCormick of McCormick & Co. were among the speakers.

According to the 1975 conference brochure, "Few executives can say they've grabbed the reins of a struggling company and turned it around. But Charles P. 'Buzz' McCormick Jr. did it—twice—with the company that bears his family name. Not many, including McCormick himself, would have predicted this success. For starters, during a self-described 'rebellious' period in his teens, McCormick vowed that he would do something other than work for the company his great-uncle had founded and his father had run. That feeling was short-lived. But even when he decided to make McCormick & Co. his career, Buzz McCormick didn't expect to one day run the world's largest spice maker."

Other headliners took the podium at home in ACG Toronto's early

days, including Frank Stronach, an Austrian-Canadian who founded
Magna International, an international automotive parts company,
and Magna Entertainment Corp., which specializes in horseracing
entertainment. (Magna won the ACG Outstanding Corporate Growth
Award in 1996.)

Canadian-US Tie Stronger with Coach

Coach Coffey had strong ties with US business. He was elected
president of ACG Global in fall 1979 and took over the reins in 1980 as
the first non-US ACG president. (He continues to hold that distinction.)
Coach worked with Carroll Greathouse's firm in Connecticut, ACG's
first management company. His support of InterGrowth never flagged,
and he was a consummate salesman; the 1980 InterGrowth in San
Diego felt the effects of the Canadian president with a swelling of
attendance from Toronto!

*Bob Coffey attended each InterGrowth from 1972 until he severed his quadriceps
tendon in the spring of 2000.*

Corder Provides Administrative Heft

Barbara Corder, who worked for Mr. Coffey at Ernst & Whinney
starting in 1979, became a key player in ACG Toronto. In those days, the
chapter was referred to the as the Canadian Association for Corporate
Growth. *(It retained that title until brand guidelines adopted in 2004
forced an end to all identities other than ACG.)*

Part of Ms. Corder's job was devoted to organizing ACG in Toronto.
"I just jumped in," she recalled. "Bob [Coffey] gave the overview and
handed me the work. I sat with the chapter board, did brainstorming,
made lots of calls to pull in good speakers right from the get-go.

"Even after Bob and I had left Ernst & Whinney, we still were
involved with ACG Toronto while employed at ABM-Amro Bank. He
certainly was the lynchpin of the chapter for more than twenty years.

"There was loyalty in Toronto. At least 50 percent of core members renewed every year, but fortunately, there was also turnover with fresh blood. Bob was a strong recruiter for many years. After a while, we needed more.

"I remember when Renate Herbst of Bennett Jones Verchere came on board later and lent her muscle to revitalizing the chapter."

Herbst Provides Insight into Development

Ms. Herbst joined ACG Toronto in 1986. She looked back at the fifteen years from 1986 to 2001, when all monthly meetings were held on the same Tuesday at the Albany Club and recalled, "There were no women attendees other than me until the 1990s. The chapter was an old boys' network. It continued to attract good speakers, many of whom became leading Canadian business magnates. The board had little turnover and was self-selected."

"ACG Toronto was in debt in the early 2000s and generating no sustainable income. Several of the directors stepped up and prepaid for events and advanced dues to sustain us. ACG Global helped us out by forgiving payment of dues for a period of time. This allowed ACG Toronto to achieve fiscal viability.

"Another go-getter on the board who became president at the turn of the century was Jason Sparaga of Spara Capital Partners, Inc. He and I made an attempt to sunset the board and bring on known business leaders. The momentum of ACG branding and the ACG Capital Connection became excellent selling points to assist us in attracting new persons to the board. Carl Wangman and Charlie Downer attended a meeting in Toronto of the potential board members to assist our cause.

"About this time, I was on the branding committee of ACG Global and was thrilled when we decided to use ACG Toronto as the template chapter for the rollout of the brand. This decision helped reduce administrative costs and brought us to the forefront of ACG during a period of seminal change."

Ms. Herbst recalled the importance of the ACG Capital Connection. "With the advent of the first Toronto ACG Capital Connection, we had funds and were finally a great chapter. We used the ACG Global model in many respects. "We benefited from the many changes and advances made at ACG Global. At the same time, we stopped the monthly meetings at the Albany Club and began a new set of programs, which included deal marts, breakfasts, different dinner venues, and social events, including golf."

More Drive, New Insights: Sparaga and Amadori Lead

Dan Amadori, ACG Toronto president in 2010, embraced many of the sentiments of Ms. Herbst. "The chapter hit a low approximately ten years ago, and its financial resources dwindled to the point that its ongoing success was in question. In 2000, Jason Sparaga became chapter president. Over the next several years, he recruited a number of new board members, most of whom continue to serve as board members currently.

"The breakthrough for the Toronto chapter was its inaugural ACG Capital Connection of 2003," said Mr. Amadori of Lamerac Financial Corp. "This was pulled together over a period of several months. Jay Jester, who was one of the pioneers of the ACG Capital Connection in the US, coached the organizing committee from ACG Toronto.

"The event attracted more than three hundred people, some new sponsorship funds for the organization, and gave it, most importantly, immediate recognition in the Toronto marketplace."

Don Amadori, President ACG Toronto, at Capital Connection, June 15, 2006

Mr. Amadori was recruited to serve on the board as "president-in-waiting" in 2004 and took over as president in 2005. He recalled, "We needed to create a sustainable value-added proposition for the chapter.

We started to create events that were meaningful and memorable. The first year we focused activity on the ACG Capital Connection by adding events of note. We launched board strategy sessions and an annual half-day retreat. We began to develop better governance procedures, committee charters, and mandatory attendance rules for board members at meetings and events. We did not, however, change our dues structure, because we felt we needed to build more value.

"The first event of significance was a 'Manufacturing in Canada Symposium' that attracted approximately three hundred people—executives and bankers—interested in learning how a businessman had successfully challenged the Chinese manufacturing juggernaut in the World Trade Organization on an anti-dumping case. Over dinner, he explained how he won his case at great cost and effort. The press was there, and the chapter earned many accolades. Photos from the event gave us the opportunity to create a photo gallery on our website. It was a complete success.

"We set a modest target of three dinner meetings per year as part of our go-forward calendar. In each case, a sponsor was secured, and the presentation involved a successful transaction between the private-equity community and the investee company," continued Mr. Amadori. "We also marketed the event by asking the board members to make personal calls and sending e-mail notices to our expanding member/prospect list."

Collaborative Programs Builds Brand

"We focused on building this list—in 2005, it included fewer than five hundred people, and over the next five years, we have expanded it to five thousand. We did this by working with a number of other organizations—the Canadian Manufacturing Association, various boards of trade, Canadian Venture Capital Association, Financial Executives Institute, etc. We organized co-branded events with some of these groups, a decision that helped entrench the ACG Toronto profile in the business community.

"In 2006, we began to look for more new events that would distinguish our chapter. We introduced an annual Super Bowl party in late January—a feel-good event in a downtown location with raffle prizes, local sports celebrities as our guests, the Toronto Argonauts football cheerleaders, a progressive round of poker with five tables, etc.

It has become the early winter season social event on the calendar and currently attracts a crowd of more than three hundred people."

ACG Toronto Annual General Meeting, June 15, 2006

Second ACG Capital Connection, CEO Golf Tourney, Charitable Donation

"We began to investigate options and alternatives to round out our by now highly successful ACG Capital Connection. In 2009, we launched the Canadian Debt & Equity Forum, a hybrid of the ACG Capital Connection that has more of a US private equity flavor. This event is restricted to financial institutions that have an established presence in Canada.

"We have found that by augmenting our ACG Capital Connection with this 'Made in Canada' capital showcase, we have catered to a much larger range of business organizations that are attracted to the event.

"One of the missing ingredients was the ongoing commitment of business executives to become members of our chapter. On that basis, we launched a different format for our golf tournament by tailoring it to the CEO community. We have held four annual golf tournaments—the 'ACG Golf Classics.' We invite approximately fifty CEOs as guests to the tournament, which features a gala luncheon and keynote address by an executive from a high-profile charity. In the past four years, we have showcased the Toronto Argonauts' 'Stop the Violence' charitable initiative, the Heart & Stroke Foundation, and the United Way. The tournament net proceeds are donated to these charities, approximately $10,000 for each worthy cause. This initiative has enhanced the profile of ACG within the Toronto business executive community.

"The common theme in all of this is ensuring that our programming is known for its high quality. We have worked hard at building each event, filling the room, and offering value to attendees."

Jim Flaherty, Canadian Minister of Finance, speaking at ACG Toronto Capital Connection, November 15, 2007

Noteworthy Outcomes—More Revenue, Leadership

"The results are noticeable—the chapter has attracted substantial new sponsorship and is financially solvent, with cash reserves in excess of one year's operating budget. While we struggled with fewer than fifty active members ten years ago, we now have sixty members on committees and a robust membership of approximately two hundred fifty members. We have programming, membership, governance, special events, golf, ACG Capital Connection, Debt & Equity, and nominations committees managed by a fifteen-person board and lead volunteers.

"The next steps for the Toronto chapter are to engage more resources, so as to develop a comprehensive marketing approach and program content. The chapter has invested thousands of dollars in upgrading its information systems and databases and continues to market aggressively in the Toronto area, across Ontario and increasingly into North America.

We have actively participated at InterGrowth and have promoted a number of large Canadian organizations and companies that have become sponsors of the chapter and InterGrowth."

"It's a new day in ACG Toronto!"

ACG Toronto Breakfast Seminar Speaker-Laurie Turnbull, Artemus Group, and Dan Amadori, President ACG Toronto

CHAPTER 8

ACG Los Angeles

1972
FOUNDER DISAPPEARS, CHAPTER RALLIES

The first president of the Los Angeles chapter was John Castellucci, according to the 1972 InterGrowth brochure. Mr. Castellucci, employed by Cardiff Industries, quickly lost interest in ACG and after his term moved away.

"He never showed up at an L.A. meeting again," recalled Paul Johnson of Hoover, Johnson & Co., who was president of the chapter in 1976. There is no further mention of Mr. Castellucci in later discussions with chapter pioneers. There is abundant evidence, however, the chapter was up and running by 1972.

Jonathan Club First Venue

The chapter held its first meetings at the Jonathan Club in downtown Los Angeles. Dick Israel, president of the chapter from 1998–2000, remembers the early meetings. "We always had a speaker, and the meetings were always luncheons. About seventy-five people attended. I personally found the downtown locale too far from my office; so much time away from the office was not productive," said Mr. Israel of Dick Israel & Partners.

Jim Blaising, who was ACG Global president in 1988–1989, also recalled the early meetings. "I attended the early meetings. At two or three meetings, there were discussions on how to do something in the business—to talk a little more about the principles of a merger or acquisition. People were not doing them like they are now in 2010. It was a relatively new activity in the business community." He added, "Then I was a business appraiser with American Appraisal Associates, Inc."

Struggle to Attract "Corporates"

"ACG was a good organization to help develop business and offer counsel to the corporations. There was no reservation in letting me into the chapter because it was the service people who made the chapter work. It was always a problem getting the corporate people involved."

The service providers went at it. John Heath, an executive with Marshall & Stevens, Inc., became the second chapter president. A fellow employee, Carl Hagelin, Mike Moy of KPMG, and Hal Harrigian of Duff & Phelps are mentioned as driving forces behind the fledgling chapter. Neill Lawton followed Mr. Heath as president. Mr. Lawton was the manager of the industrial department of Security National Bank.

These were bankers, valuations experts, and other service providers, the movers and shakers who carried the mantle for the new chapter.

Paul Johnson, membership chairman under Mr. Heath, recalls a move for the Los Angeles chapter to drop out of ACG.

"During Neill's administration, we were considering dropping out of ACG to become only a local association because, to a group out in California, the national ACG did not seem to be worth the dues invested. The national ACG president, Tony Haas of AgriCapital Corp., came out during his term, 1975–1976, to see us and convinced us to stay with the national organization," said Mr. Johnson, who would win the ACG Meritorious Service Award in 1993.

"It was after I started attending InterGrowth that the value of a national organization became more significant."

The '70s, a Balancing Act

Corporate Members Take Lead from Service Providers in Steady-Growth Decade

In 1976, under Mr. Johnson's presidency, the chapter totaled fifty-six members. More than half were corporate members, and according to ACG records, some were building conglomerate businesses. There is no mention of private equity group members.

According to Mr. Johnson, "The chapter grew slowly by intent. The board worked hard at recruiting corporate executives and admitted only those service providers that had significant responsibility in their organizations and fit with our group.

"We tried to avoid having too much competition between service firms or accepting service members who would aggressively buttonhole corporate members for business purposes. We worked hard at maintaining good programs with educational value. We had a collegial atmosphere and very good attendance."

Late '70s, Early '80s Membership Drops Off

In 1980, ACG Los Angeles was struggling for growth with 143 members. By 1981, the chapter dropped to 130 members. Mr. Johnson recalls frequent visitors from San Francisco, San Diego, Phoenix, and other markets that eventually established their own chapters. Howard Vultee of Merrill Lynch was one of those who established the San Francisco chapter in 1976. It enjoyed success almost immediately.

Mr. Johnson remembered the same scenario. "We had some reservations about encouraging an Orange County chapter because it would cut into our membership, but we did so anyway. Some years after that, the San Diego chapter was formed."

Jim Blaising, ACG Global president from 1988–1989, remembered helping in the formation of the Orange County and San Diego chapters. A member of the Los Angeles chapter, Mr. Blaising also recalled "a disconnect between international ACG and chapters. Chapters didn't know what international was. We really didn't have a strong organization in terms of the international headquarters. It kind of held the chapters together and accommodated InterGrowth."

By 1990, membership in the Los Angeles chapter had dipped to ninety-eight. The decline may have been sparked by the emergence of new chapters nearby that "stole" members from Los Angeles. In fact, the number of members from the three new chapters in San Francisco, Orange County, and San Diego increased to 216 by 1990. Their growth probably depleted Los Angeles's membership rolls.

Late '80s: Tough Economy Impacts Chapter

Franz von Bradsky of Green Tree Capital recounted the chapter's early years in a difficult economy, confirming the focus on corporate members.

"I discovered the Los Angeles chapter in the mid '80s. It did not advertise, and it didn't want service providers. I finally got onto the

Los Angeles board in the late '80s. I remember in 1991 we had a small conference in L.A., which was the first full-day ACG conference in the West. It has evolved to become almost as large as InterGrowth.

"The economy was crummy. We were losing thousands of aerospace jobs paying thirty-five dollars an hour. In the San Fernando Valley, the number of homes for sale skyrocketed. [One] couldn't get a moving van because all of them were heading to the Midwest. A friend of mine bought a house in Thousand Oaks and didn't recover financially for ten years.

"The savings-and-loan crisis started in '89. More businesses went belly-up in Southern California and Arizona.

"While I was president of ACG Los Angeles in 1992, we held the second full-day conference, but membership did not grow appreciably. We always compared ourselves to San Francisco, which had about twenty to thirty more members. There were more service members in L.A. and more corporates in San Francisco.

"I increased the chapter board from nine or ten members to twenty-three. In this way, each board member could be given a small assignment and be expected to complete it. I could beat up on them if they didn't do it. My thinking was that if more people were active on the board, retention would improve. I started the committee structure, but on balance we were neither hurting nor growing."

Service Providers Gain Strength; The "Celebrity Effect"

The Los Angeles Venture Association (LAVA) had an impact on the continuing development of ACG Los Angeles. Four former LAVA presidents: Joe Wingard of Merrill Lynch; Mr. von Bradsky; Dave Morgan, partner in Barton Klugman & Oetting; and Mr. Israel breathed new life into the chapter.

In the fall of 1997, the chapter began planning for a new kind of one-day conference, spearheaded by Mr. Wingard, Jim Friedman of Barrington Associates, and Jeri Harman of Allied Capital. Mr. Israel, who would assume the presidency in 1998, reflected on their efforts.

"They pushed the big conference idea through the board, which was fearful of losing money the chapter didn't have. But it was successful from the start—it made money. The keys to success were luminary speakers outside the chapter—like the late and legendary coach John Wooden and the late Walter Cronkite."

Continued Mr. Israel, "It went from a one-day to two-day event at the Beverly Hills Hotel to the larger Beverly Hilton with eight hundred attendees. The celebrity effect of Southern California turned the tide. in 2010 the ACG Capital Connection got 1,400 attendees and 130 exhibitors.

"We continued to change the programs at ACG Los Angeles to bring in more name speakers and attention-getting venues," said Mr. Israel. "For example, when Staples Center opened, we made arrangements for a tour and lunch there. Now Staples is well known, but then it was a big deal. Another time, we met in Dodger Stadium, had a tour of the dugout and field, followed by lunch. Members were impressed."

Mr. Israel lists the following as key things chapter leaders did to influence the success of the chapter:

- Decided to bring in name speakers instead of good topics. "For example, we brought two speakers from New York—Paul Rossetti of American Securities Capital Partners and John Huey of Time, Inc."

- Enabled close networking among the group, "a pattern that we first started at LAVA in 1985. Everyone stood up and introduced himself in a thirty-second elevator speech with a microphone so everyone could hear. This was critical to a familial feeling."

- Copied all business cards of attendees and sent them around to the entire group after the meeting.

- Employed an executive director.

- Developed the ACG Cup with many others in the chapter, such as Steve Appel of Gregory & Appel Insurance (in 2011) and Doug Schreier of Deloitte & Touche, LLC.

- Built in sponsorship throughout our programs.

Speaker Michael Eisner (former Chairman of Disney) at ACG Los Angeles

Speaker George Stephanopoulos (former President Clinton adviser and TV personality) at ACG Los Angeles 2007

L.A. Lakers Coach Phil Jackson speaks before
ACG Los Angeles audience in 2004

Programming in the Twenty-first Century Takes Off

Annual Business Conference Driving Force;
Service-Corporate Conundrum Continues

Michael Carr, partner of BAC Investments, LLC, chapter president
from 2004–2006, shared his views about the status of ACG Los Angeles
then.

"From its origins thirteen years ago, the annual ACG Los Angeles
Business Conference generated great awareness of the chapter and has
since become its financial engine. The chapter's core monthly programs
rotate from breakfast meetings in West Los Angeles to downtown early-
evening gatherings. This pattern accommodates the geographic challenges
presented by the Los Angeles basin. The chapter also has a social side, with
its large holiday party and a member-only beach party."

Bridge to other Markets

"The L.A. chapter has begun holding a series of events targeted
at specific member groups," said Mr. Carr. "There is a private equity
series for senior private equity professionals designed to encourage more

involvement by our private equity members, as well as to introduce the benefits of ACG to non-member private equity professionals."

Mr. Carr continued, "We also added a series of events tailored to corporate executives. While the majority of our members are investment professionals and service providers, we have found an underserved market with corporate executives who manage private equity-owned businesses. Lastly, we started a meeting series entitled, *Women in Growth Investing,* as the L.A. chapter continues to focus on diversity."

Speaker Mitt Romney, ACG Los Angeles 2010

Speaker Colin Powell (former U.S. Secretary of State)
at ACG Los Angeles gathering in 2005

Condolezza Rice (former U.S. Secretary of State)
addresses ACG Los Angeles audience

ACG Cup Begins in L.A.

The first ACG Cup was held in Los Angeles in tandem with three business schools. The founders envisioned that it could become a national program for ACG, and they were prescient.

Backdrop to ACG Los Angeles Cup

ACG Los Angeles kicked off 2006 with the successful launch of the ACG L.A. Cup, a case-study competition that awarded $20,000 in prizes to smart and lucky MBA students.

The Cup was created to introduce the community's future business leaders to ACG Los Angeles and its members, promote knowledge in the area of mergers and acquisitions, and strengthen the relationships between ACG and the area's leading graduate business schools: UCLA's Anderson School of Management, USC's Marshall School of Business, and Pepperdine's Graziadio School of Business and Management.

ACG Los Angeles had for several years sought an effective vehicle to reach out to today's busy MBA students when it landed on the idea of the Cup. "Our inaugural competition was a tremendous success," noted ACG Los Angeles board member Steve Appel, chairman of the event.

"The participation of 154 MBA students comprising 39 teams and more than 30 ACG Los Angeles members as judges far exceeded our expectations. The dedicated student leaders at each school took the platform and ran with it. The students were intelligent, insightful, and articulate. They will make terrific ACG members in the future."

Preliminary rounds were held at each of the three schools, with the winning team from each school competing in the finals. The four competitions were judged by five-person panels of M&A professionals, all members of the chapter.

The contest simulated a real-world experience. ACG Los Angeles board member Scott Kolbrenner, a senior vice president at Houlihan Lokey Howard & Zukin, wrote a complex, twenty-eight-page case study about a public company with a depressed stock price that receives an unsolicited offer to be acquired by a large competitor. The case study included company background information, market data, and numerous spreadsheets.

The student teams, taking the roles of investment bankers, were given a limited period of time to review the materials and fifteen minutes to "pitch" their analyses and services to represent the company. The judges, serving as the company's board of directors, challenged the teams' findings, which required both corporate finance and valuation skills.

"It was rewarding to participate in the first ACG Los Angeles Cup," said Kolbrenner. "The students, faculty, and administration at the schools all took the case-study competition seriously, perhaps due to the natural friendly rivalries between the schools, along with the carrot of $20,000 in prize money to the top three finalists."

In 2011 the ACG Cup took place in twenty-nine chapters. "ACG Cup really is charitable in nature," said Mr. Carr. "When we first started talking to schools about holding the ACG Cup, several of the schools were reluctant. ACG Los Angeles then agreed to make a $100,000 grant—$20,000 per year over five years—to be awarded to participating schools. That decision really started what is now a nationwide chapter program."

NOTE: As of 2010, ACG Los Angeles had more than six hundred members, an increase of nearly 400 percent since the turn of the century.

CHAPTER 9

MEMBERSHIP & CHAPTER GROWTH: THE STORY

ACG Members

In 1973—More than five hundred
In 2011—More than fourteen thousand

ACG Chapters

In 1973—Four
In 2011—Fifty-seven

> *One of the first references to total ACG membership came from the InterGrowth promotional brochure of 1973. "The Association for Corporate Growth now has more than 500 members representing leading corporations, investment institutions and consulting firms." The official counting of members (those who are recorded as having paid their dues) began in 1976, eight years after Chicago was officially named a "chapter."*

Changing Role for ACG Global in Building Membership

ACG took on a limited role during the 1970s and 1980s in making new chapters and helping existing ones to grow. Chapters grew more or less "naturally" through members and friends who moved from one city to another and wanted to continue the ACG experience by forming a hub in the new locale.

By 1972, four chapters were on board: New York, Chicago, Toronto, and Los Angeles. By 1979, there were 12, and membership totaled 1,570, a jump of about 300 percent in both members and chapters. Additional chapters had bubbled up in Arizona, Atlanta, Boston, Dallas-Fort Worth, Houston, Minnesota, Philadelphia, and San Francisco. As the 1980s began, ACG was gaining a foothold in North America.

By 2011, things had changed. Today ACG Global provides extensive support for chapter membership development. Chapters are now provided with membership recruitment support and prospecting. Customizable brochures are provided by ACG Global, along with consulting to assist in developing membership recruitment campaigns.

Strong Volunteers Delivered Quality, Prompted Growth

First President Sets Guiding Principles

Thomas F. Smith of Ernst & Ernst, the first president of ACG, recalled the purpose of ACG. "We were simply trying to connect with business colleagues we could trust. We wanted to find folks that would share what it takes to make a deal. That trust was the rock upon which we began to build our network.

"Back then," he continued, "ACG was New York. When we formed ACG Chicago in 1968 and ACG Toronto in 1971 and ACG Los Angeles by 1972, the association was more than New York. Being an ACG member opened doors to other members. We really had faith in and trusted each other."

First President Carries the Flag

Mr. Smith, who late in life lost both legs to the ravages of diabetes and required a wheelchair and full-time caregiver, spoke his mind about ACG loud and clear. A Hoosier himself, he, his caregiver, and ACG Executive Director Carl Wangman drove together to Indianapolis in 2004 when ACG Indiana was chartered.

Mr. Wangman recalls Mr. Smith's excitement when he realized that more than one hundred men and women had already joined the chapter before its inaugural meeting.

"The first ACG president sped around the venue in his motorized chair, greeting any and all," said Mr. Wangman. "Later, when asked to address the group, Mr. Smith said, 'Ladies and gentlemen, I am delighted to share in this event. Over forty years ago, when I first became involved with ACG, we had a simple objective: we wanted to find folks we could trust to discuss how the deal business works. There were only a handful of us. Today there are over seven thousand ACG members ... all built on trust, so please, from this old fart ... don't f*&% it up.'"

Who Connects the Dots?

If ACG Global played such a minor role in chapter development in the early years, which volunteers sustained the association?

No doubt about it. The service providers—intermediaries, lawyers, bankers, accountants, valuation experts and other consultants—who handled key components of the deal process also pushed for new chapters. They may not have been the intrepid travelers on the old Silk Road, but they were the dealmakers who carried the message about ACG. They found value in networking at ACG meetings. They listened hard to top corporate executives sharing their "war stories." They joined and took the lead in ACG's expansion.

Eventually it became a problem. Service providers overloaded the association, but not right away.

Balancing Membership Growth Growing Concern

Donald Reed, who was with National Can Corp. when he was ACG president from 1976–1977, recalled, "All chapters were growing well as the organization became more widely known. Our heavy membership of corporate officers and management seemed to be an incentive for the services (accounting, lawyers, banking, consultants, etc.) to become interested, and I recall board meeting discussions about how to achieve a more balanced membership."

Then, when an ACG member traveled beyond his or her chapter, there was no easy way to connect with other ACG members. The first ACG membership directory was produced in 1978. It contained 89 pages that covered 1,300 members from 1,083 companies. "It was well received by the members," said Mr. Reed.

Balancing the membership mix of corporates, service providers, and intermediaries began soon after ACG's founding days and continued for decades. Gary Fiebert, ACG president in 1982–1983, senior vice president of Find/SVP, Inc., echoed the sentiment.

"One concern that stands out was the need to balance the role of members from service provider organizations (accountants, consultants, investment banks, and the like) with the objectives of the corporate members (networking for deal opportunities). I recall that this topic received a lot of attention at these gatherings, and striking that balance served me well throughout the rest of my career."

A few years later, Walt Howiler, ACG president from 1985–1986, recalled the same concern. "There was the corporate-service conundrum I always was considering or grappling with," said the executive with Kirk Paper, who expressed other needs as well.

"When I was president, ACG finances were not certain; there was a part-time management office in Chicago, and the national group did not do much except host InterGrowth. When an ACG member left his homeport to travel to another city, there was no easy way to locate other members and meetings.

"The culture of trust was always important, even though we were a loose federation," said Mr. Howiler. "There was the trust. Friendships blossomed, and they kept us together."

Holding It Together Becomes Challenge as New Chapters Develop

Between Messrs. Fiebert's and Howiler's presidencies, Harry Fendrich of CAM Interests also recalled during his ACG term (1983–1984) that ACG wanted to expand but struggled for unity.

"We strongly supported the development of a new chapter in Silicon Valley. We also looked to several other cities for new chapters, including international locales beyond Toronto. Strengthening the ACG chapter 'confederacy' was an important focus of our international efforts.

"We worked to demonstrate value of the overall organization largely through the excellent speakers and programs at the InterGrowth conference and the expansion of the membership directory, which was very useful for business deal contacts."

Who Needs a National Hub?

The thread of questionable national value weaves back to the mid-'70s.

Paul Johnson, president of ACG Los Angeles in 1976–1977, remembered, "During Neill Lawton's presidency of Los Angeles, we were considering dropping out of the ACG to just become a local association because, to a group out in California, the national ACG did not seem to be worth the dues invested.

"The national ACG president, Tony Haas, General Foods, 1975–1976, came out to see us and convinced us to stay with the national organization."

A unifying conference was key. "It was after I started attending InterGrowth that the value of a national organization became more significant," said Mr. Johnson, who was a partner in the law firm Hoover, Johnson & Company and responsible for the M&A practice.

Mr. Howiler was challenged to keep the chapters from wandering from the fold. In addition to the Los Angeles chapter, Boston expressed interest in seceding and becoming a local group.

Mr. Howiler recalled, "I talked to the leaders in both chapters and posed the question: 'Do you want to stay a nice luncheon club or create a meaningful, robust national organization?' At least for the time being, they were convinced to stay with the national group."

Global Entity Translates to InterGrowth Host

ACG President Jim Blaising (1988–1989) of American Appraisal Co., recalled a loose confederation with ACG. "ACG Global kind of held the chapters together and accommodated InterGrowth."

Mr. Blaising, active in the Los Angeles chapter, remembers efforts to expand ACG. He helped form the Orange County chapter in 1983 and the San Diego chapter in 1984 and added, "There was always that disconnect between international ACG and chapters. Chapters didn't know what international was." He commented on ACG President Phil Nielsen's attempt to mitigate the disconnect between ACG and chapters like Los Angeles. "Phil tried to get some common practices shared among chapters through communication tools like the *ACG Journal for Corporate Growth.*"

Facing Up: Attitude Turnaround

In the late '80s and into the '90s, ACG Global leadership began to take determined steps to heal the disconnect and strengthen the relationship with existing chapters. ACG faced the issue of membership criteria that differed from chapter to chapter. The Global board created a policy that grandfathered membership—allowing ACG members to transfer from one chapter to another without losing their membership—to help solve the nagging problem. And ACG Global tackled the need for a comprehensive approach to assist chapters in building membership.

The efforts began to pay off. By the end of the 1980s, ACG

experienced a steady net growth of about a thousand members. In 10 years, its ranks increased from 1,570 to 2,621 members. It now had twenty-one chapters, nearly doubling the number of chapters from a decade before.

Exploring New Avenues for Growth

During the first half of the '90s, ACG Global Vice President of Membership Debbie Victory stressed new recruitment activities for chapters. Chapter cooperation began to grow as never before with Ms. Victory of the Akron Regional Development Board, who took examples of the more imaginative chapters and shared them throughout the organization.

Her "VictoryGrams" included ideas like meeting collaborations with similar organizations, such as the Turnaround Management Association, the Financial Executives Institute, and business school alumni groups. She encouraged co-branded events, promotional collaboration, and membership list swaps. She wrote about successful recruiting strategies, introduced the first membership growth contest between chapters, and circulated a chapter self-audit guide that she had drafted.

Chapter Development Requires Standardization, Individualization, Patience

Mr. Wangman remembered giving new chapter organizers elaborate guidelines—a virtual road map on best practices for chapter formation. He encouraged a new board position for vice president of new chapter development who worked side by side with the vice president of membership. The board liked the idea.

In the mid- to late 1990s, ACG Global leaders and staff concentrated on North American and European areas for new chapters.

"The road to a new chapter was never short," said Mr. Wangman. "Our first visit to Indianapolis in 1995 to the actual chartering of ACG Indiana took nine years. For ACG Frankfurt, it took eleven."

The painstaking process of chartering a new chapter was also reflected in the process of acquiring and maintaining new corporate members.

During the tenure of Clark Childers of Offutt Childers Putnam,

P.C., who was ACG Global membership vice president from 1994–1997, ACG Global headquarters obtained a list of three thousand directors of corporate development and circulated it to the chapters. ACG Global marketing developed "corporate" recruitment materials and provided them to chapters at no cost.

Balance in Motion

The balance of membership—corporate/service/private equity—hadn't gone away then and hasn't yet today totally. ACG Denver, a chapter with a history of serving corporate members, principally because private equity was not as present in the city, still puts the corporate/service balance at the forefront.

Said Clifford R. Pearl of Hensley Kim & Holzer, LLC., of Denver, "The balance of corporate and service providers is an issue.

"Denver does not have a large PEG community," said the ACG Global director, who is also the chapter's vice president of corporate member affairs. "Getting the corporate folks to participate is an ongoing struggle."

The corporate breakfasts went dark for about a year, but they have been rekindled. Now we have a corporate membership that is a premium rate that allows four members of the organization to have ACG membership privileges. Not a globally recognized program, just locally. A few other chapters are doing this, and now it is on the global agenda.

"Now we are also creating mechanism to do an affirmative outreach to Denver's corporate membership called Corporate Plus, yet it is still difficult to get corporate members to attend. Monthly luncheons are the chapter's primary events with more than two hundred attendees, mostly CEOs of companies with revenues in excess of $50 million. We've upgraded the content and seen a rise in attendance.

"We also have initiated separate breakfast meetings for members and guests who are corporate CEOs of companies with revenue of $5 million and up."

ACG Does a Retake on Chapters ... New and Revitalized

Robb Offers Cure for "Sick" Chapters

Russ Robb of O'Conor Wright Wyman, Inc., in Boston, assumed the office of vice president of membership in 1997 following Mr. Childers. Mr. Robb reaffirmed the importance of setting chapter membership goals and keeping in touch with the chapter leaders. He stressed having a strategy for the chapter's membership campaign. He also believed in having monthly meetings so there was no gap in attention to members.

Mr. Robb earned a reputation for directness. "If your chapter is failing, try harder. If you have failed at building membership, try tact. Change the board, change the president, change the venue, change the program format, change the time of the meeting. If you don't have an administrator, get one!"

He continued, "One of my favorite heroes was Bear Bryant, the legendary coach of the Alabama football team. At half time he would say, 'Go out there and hit somebody…make a tackle…make a fumble… make something happen.'"

Membership Growth over Ten Years

From 1990 to 2000, ACG membership jumped approximately 100 percent, from 2,544 to 5,054. One-third of the increase came from ten new chapters during the 1990s. The twenty-four chapters that existed in 1990 experienced significant growth, with more than a 100 percent spike from the following nine chapters:

Orange County	510%
Boston	333%
National Capital	291%
South Florida	262%
Silicon Valley	247%
St. Louis	208%
Charlotte	192%
Detroit	144%
Philadelphia	100%

The growth stories of the above ACG chapters center on the quality of leadership. New leaders help to refocus the chapter. Changes in programming, experimenting with different venues and meeting times, marketing and outreach, expanding the size and involvement of the board, engaged membership recruiting—all led these chapters to accelerated growth.

New Chapters Require Strong Leaders on the Ground

Of the late '90s, John Gullman of GSR Partners recalled, "All efforts collapsed if we didn't have the strong leader on the ground. We needed a small core of committed individuals who saw the value of ACG for their careers or professional development. They, in turn, needed to convince their colleagues of the value proposition. Without these essential elements (and the commitment of time and money by ACG Global board and its staff), we would never have received the big payoff in the first years of the twenty-first century, when membership and the number of chapters dramatically increased. ACG Global brought in resources of money and talent."

Gullman Describes Advances in South Florida

Jester Recalls Glenn Oken's Grace

Until he attended an ACG regional meeting, Mr. Gullman did not sense the enormity of the global organization. "We sat around a horseshoe at my first regional chapter leadership meeting, and I was extremely impressed with the Boston chapter. This is a great organization, I thought. When you walk away from an ACG meeting, you get a great feeling. It got me enthused about how things were run.

"Carl Wangman and I spoke about the South Florida chapter, which I took over as president… I told him running the chapter was like Vietnam, where we got overrun each night but were alive the following day to fight on. Carl had come down on a fact-finding mission a few months earlier, to see if the chapter should keep going. So when I returned to South Florida, I re-assembled the board, found a chapter administrator, got some good people involved, and began to interest our members in our programs. We were on our way. We started a nice trend upward.

"Later in 1996, someone asked me if I would do domestic chapter development. That was my first real job on the ACG Global board. Tampa was the first one I had a hand in getting off the ground. I worked with Jay Jester, Florida Capital Partners (FCP)."

Mr. Jester remembered the experience as well. "I had just joined Glenn Oken at FCP, and one of the first marketing events he took me to was an InterGrowth event in Orlando—I have not missed an InterGrowth since," said Mr. Jester.

"Glenn knew everyone in the room and treated ACG like his extended family. Oken continues to be a role model for me in the role of business development. To me, he embodies the character of an ACG member. Every event he attends, he leads with a generous spirit and a genuine interest in whomever he's talking to or meeting with. As a young private equity professional, I remember being impressed that Glenn would spend 75 percent of the meeting trying to find ways to help the other person. He'd save his need, his request, his acquisition interest for the end.

"His model of give first, ask last was a powerful example for me."

Mr. Gullman mentioned other chapters he bolstered or helped ignite. "In Denver, I was involved with [staff members] Carl Wangman, Judy Iacuzzi, and ACG Denver member Bob Prangley, who was with CFA Associates, in restarting the Denver chapter. I also had a hand in the Kansas City start-up with Jim O'Donnell, Capital for Business, Inc.

"ACG Western Michigan was spearheaded by Tom Doyal, Plante & Moran, whom I had met in Florida. Again and again, veteran ACG members who moved to new jobs in areas without ACG chapters were leaders in forming new chapters. In looking at sites for ACG chapters, I thought if there were a metropolitan area that supported four professional sports, we needed to have a chapter there. Those were the criteria … baseball, football, hockey, and basketball. That's worked out well in most places.

"Education and relationships of quality are the draw, including private equity guys. They attend ACG meetings, and it's a who's-who in the deal business. Find a couple of people who are charismatic … who are willing to start the chapter … and then you get other people who are willing to make it grow."

Coping with Rapid-Fire Growth

Few were prepared for the growth in chapters the first years of the twenty-first century: twenty in all, including two Canadian (Calgary and Vancouver) and five European (Austria, France, Frankfurt, Holland, and Rhine-Ruhr). The European chapters' gestation (from the first official contact of ACG Global headquarters to the first month of dues payments to ACG Global) averaged ten years during the mid-'90s, when David Love of Ray & Berndtson was the ACG vice president of international development.

The average gestation period for chapters in the States was about four years. There were exceptions. The possibility of chapters in Connecticut and New Jersey was discussed by ACG New York as early as the mid-'80s and didn't materialize until 2001 and 2003 respectively.

The growth of twenty new chapters and a net increase of nearly five thousand members over five years brought with it challenges that ACG had not faced before. One issue was to devote time and attention to a unifying brand. The look of ACG, its identity at the time, was a hodgepodge. A mottled identity led to confusion in the marketplace and threatened ACG's first-tier reputation.

Jeri Harman of Allied Capital Corp., veteran leader of both ACG Global and ACG Los Angeles, explained, "ACG recognized the need to become more of a high-quality name within the business community, and branding was the key way to get there on a global and consistent basis. Consistency in look and message was key."

From 2009–2011, chapter development became yet more standardized and supported by ACG Global professional staff. Chapters in Nebraska and Kentucky took just a year from initial contact to achieve sustainable operations with one hundred-plus members. In the space of two years, chapters were formed in China, Spain, and the Czech Republic.

New Strategies Boost Internationalism

Late in the first decade of the twenty-first century, ACG Global re-asserted the importance of global growth. Den White, ACG chairman in 2009–2010, described it.

"We continue to grow beyond US borders. With Patrick Hurley's leadership, we became partners with the city of Tianjin in China. We have set up an entity in China with its own board.

"A new chapter has also been formed in the Czech Republic," continued Mr. White of Verrill Dana LLP. "We continue to explore new chapters in Europe and have set our strategy for India. We are keenly aware of how different restrictions in many countries influence how we approach ACG's outreach into those areas."

Michael Carr Addresses International Growth Issues

According to Michael Carr, chairman of ACG 2010–2011, "One of our goals is to better connect our North American chapters with our chapters around the world. We found that more than 50 percent of our members expect to increase their cross-border business over the next five years, and ACG needed to take steps in assisting its members in this area."

Mr. Carr, of BAC Investments, Inc., described one step taken to improve the connection with ACG's European chapters—the European Advisory Council (EAC) developed in 2010. "The EAC was created to assist our seven European chapters in working together and to foster better communication with ACG Global. The Council gives ACG the tools to more easily clarify substantive issues," said the chairman.

He continued, "The M&A market has become more vibrant in China. In establishing ACG in China, we drew upon the Tianjin Municipal Government and the China International Private Equity Conference (CIPEF), which ACG co-sponsors and produces with ACG China." ACG then appointed Youming Ye of the Jordan Company to lead ACG China, and the chapter has been focused on building membership, "which will lead to everything else," said Mr. Carr.

Commenting on the ACG-China footprint, Mr. Wangman said, "Starting from the first days of the twenty-first century and the first forays into developing an ACG China chapter, no one in the organization was more instrumental in setting the course than Patrick Hurley of Mid-Market Capital Advisors, Inc., in Philadelphia.

"From his days as president of ACG Philadelphia to his chairmanship of ACG Global in 2006–2007, Patrick has been a pioneer. He orchestrated transoceanic

education seminars between Philadelphia and Hong Kong and the China mainland. He worked with Chinese leaders in Hong Kong to build his business there and create a viable chapter for ACG.

"He has worked with Andy Rice, senior vice president international business of The Jordan Company, and now Mr. Hurley's spadework—including studying the language—is paying off in an even bigger way for ACG."

Gary LaBranche, ACG President & CEO, and Cui Jin Du, Vice Mayor, Municipal Peoples Government, Tianjin, China

In commenting on The Jordan Company's role, Mr. Rice first mentioned Jordan's involvement in ACG starting in the '80s, "Over the past twenty years, more than half of all our deals at our company have involved someone from ACG, either the broker/intermediary that introduced the deal to us or a lawyer or accountant representing the seller. These relationships, nurtured through ACG, have helped us find and get deals done worldwide.

"We also have been involved in ACG chapter development. The Jordan Company helped get ACG Austria started. Torben Luth of our company sponsored several ACG events in Vienna with Harald Klien of CDI Beteiligungsberatung, which led to the formation of the chapter. Harald was its first chapter president. David W. Zalaznick, one of the managing principals of our company, co-sponsored the official inaugural meeting of ACG Austria."

Harald Klien—ACG Enthusiast

Mr. Klien was the first president of ACG Austria. It should be noted that he played a leading role in the formation of many European chapters, in particular the German, Dutch, and the latest in the Czech Republic. Mr. Klien is outspoken in his concern that European professionals take a stronger position in the growth and development of chapters in Europe.

Mr. Rice continued, "I personally was very involved in setting up the new China chapter and have supported the ACG Tianjin event.

"My colleague, Mr. Youming Ye, helped organize and host the exploratory chapter meetings in Beijing and Shanghai, which led to the formation of the ACG China chapter. Mr. Ye was appointed by the ACG Global board as the first chairman of ACG China."

ACG Global Focus Strengthens All Chapters

As ACG Global begins the second decade of the twenty-first century, it continues to focus on strengthening existing chapters. It has tightened its criteria for establishing new chapters.

ACG Global Vice President of Chapter Operations Leslie Whittet explains, "Expectations of chapter performance has evolved from the early efforts of the mid-'90s. We now have metrics that touch on all aspects of the operation of an ACG chapter, including growth expectations, programming, and leadership. They are designed to help chapters create sustainable operations and governance."

In addition, groups of chapters have come together to host cooperative regional events, such as the Tri-State meeting of New York, New Jersey, and Connecticut, and the Texas ACG Capital Connection, which added ACG Louisiana to its signature event. According to Joan McCarthy of ACG Cleveland, "We created a regional ACG Capital Connection, covering the Great Lakes area chapters: Detroit, Cincinnati, Cleveland, Indiana, Columbus, and Pittsburgh. It began in 2009. I would guess in future years other chapters will want to do this sort of regional meeting as well."

ACG President & CEO Sheds New Light on Familiar Issues

In reviewing the corporate-service member balance and bugaboo of so many global chairmen and chapter presidents in the 1980s and 1990s, Gary LaBranche, ACG president and CEO today, sheds a new light that dispels the old problem.

"Corporates are now 20 percent of ACG's fourteen thousand members—a new all-time high. Clearly there is room within ACG for corporate, service providers, and capital providers. Indeed, this diversity is perhaps ACG's greatest asset."

CHAPTER 10

VISIBILITY

EARLIEST MARKETING:
WORD OF MOUTH, BROCHURES, LOGO,
JOURNAL AND AWARDS PROGRAM

In the beginning, ACG relied on word of mouth and fliers to inform members of its plans. The most referenced message-makers in ACG archives are Peter Hilton, Tom Smith—both deceased—and Bob Coffey.

With the onset of the InterGrowth conference in 1972, brochures helped spread the news and stir up excitement. About the same time, Director Fred Roberton of Design Consultants, Inc. in Chicago designed the first black-and-green ACG logo. The arrow, as it was called, would last in various iterations for thirty years. After Peter Hilton died in 1975, the board launched a national award in his name to recognize annually a large company with top growth potential. Thirty-three companies were given the Peter Hilton Award, which later became the Outstanding Corporate Growth Award, until it was discontinued on a global level in 2009.

About a decade after the inception of the Hilton Award, in 1984, new ACG leaders created an Emerging Company Award that recognized exceptional mid-size businesses. Later, 1986 saw the launch of the first serious membership publication—*ACG Journal for Corporate Growth*—that circulated thought-leadership from chapters and InterGrowth. It lasted five years until spring 1992, when its losing financial position outweighed its other values.

Whether newspapers, radio, or television carried stories about the association's events, leaders, thought-leadership, or award-winners during the first thirty-five years is unclear. No record of systematic or even sporadic public relations work has been found. ACG may have been "the best-kept secret" from public view until the 1990s, when a new group of leaders made marketing a priority.

Association for Corporate Growth logo

ACG Journal for Corporate Growth 1989

Staff, Newsletter, New Award, Video, Brochures, and the Internet

In the first part of the '90s, after gaining stronger financial footing, ACG hired a part-time marketing director, who became full time three years later. The result was the launch of a monthly newsletter, brochures touting InterGrowth, Corporate Development Conference, and various ACG communities, such as private equity, corporate, and service members. In 1995, a postcard requesting the e-mail addresses of members was tipped into the *ACG Network* newsletter. Just three years later, electronic communication (e-mail) would become commonplace.

Market research gained traction starting in the 1990s at the InterGrowth conference. Attendees were asked to complete questionnaires. Answers to questions about the health of the marketplace and the deal activity were tabulated and dispatched in press releases for internal (ACG Network) and external media consumption. During that time, ACG started advertising—first in the *Yearbook of Experts, Authorities and Spokespersons* annual publication—and later in the *Daily Deal* and *American City Business Journals,* which ran full-page advertorials bylined by local ACG presidents, in a dozen chapter areas.

The first ACG speaker's bureau was formed, publicized, and used by members. A new member award for Meritorious Service to ACG (1992) garnered local media coverage for the recipients through press releases published by ACG Global. In 1995, ACG marketing staff wrote the script and directed videography to create a twenty-fifth anniversary InterGrowth highlight tape, which was distributed to all chapters and members as a recruitment tool.

The first gentle wave of the Internet hit in 1996 with the launch of an ACG home page developed by American Eagle, a fledgling web-developing firm in the Chicago outskirts. The home page was simple—something that "had to be done," expressed some of the leaders—of seemingly questionable value at the time. Many members did not have e-mail addresses.

The membership directory that had launched as a small-print publication in the late '70s now carried hundreds of pages, offering a fuller description of each member's work, including headshots, areas of expertise, and a cross-referencing index. Member trends surveys continued, now dispatched through the *ACG Network* to the entire membership, and the awards program highlighting three major awards was publicized locally and through a national press release through Business Wire.

In 1997, the position of vice president of online information services was added to the board and filled by George Gingerelli of the National Capital chapter. His prescient reports to the board anticipated the growth and importance of the Internet. Under Mr. Gingerelli, the home page eventually fleshed into a website that included a for-members-only section offering data previously carried in the print directory and an online deal exchange and advertising. Soon InterGrowth registration came online in 2001 for the conference held in Colorado Springs.

ACG Network Publication touts ACG InterGrowth 1991

George Gingerelli Reports to Board October 1999

"As we have mentioned on previous occasions, the ACG website should be viewed as a tool for the organization. It's a pretty good tool in its current state, but this medium suffers from rapid obsolescence. The tool must be 'sharpened' often or the users will find it 'dull' and stop using it. As acceptance for Internet-based applications (e-mail, online banking, research, e-commerce, securities trading, deal-making, etc.) grows, the business world (and, thus, our members) will demand more and more online and interactive services. While ACG is in a good position today with respect to an Internet presence, we must be prepared to offer and deliver the online services of tomorrow."

In 1998, ACG approved a program that paid for the initial creation of chapter websites with web-hosting company American Eagle Corp., and by October 1999, twenty chapters had their own sites, albeit modest in configuration. In late 1998, ACG hired a financial PR firm to focus on media coverage for chapters and InterGrowth and assist with the distribution and results of a quarterly Internet co-branded survey about the health of the deal business. (The first survey partner was Booz, Allen & Hamilton.) The PR firm FRB Financial also coordinated the first media tour of an ACG president, Conrad Tuerk, and then ACG President Chris Gebelein in 2000.

Also in 1998, ACG Global collaborated with member international firm C. Melchers Consulting to undertake a top-line growth survey, asking participation from 5,000 industry professionals that included 1,200 ACG members. It was ACG's first international survey and asked for growth trends, strategies, and corporate profiles. The 8 percent response rate made excellent content for press releases distributed nationally and internationally annually for three years.

Century Turns and ACG Becomes More Visible

In 2000, ACG Marketing Director Charles Pavia wanted to rebrand the organization, starting with a new logo. (Mr. Pavia was ahead of the curve; just three years later, ACG outsourced a wholesale branding program to one of the most influential firms in the business, Landor Associates.) In 2000, acg.org launched with a Knowledge Exchange and Resource Center that offered content on various aspects of the merger-and-acquisition business. Personalization of the website by members was introduced, and 25 percent of the membership signed on.

ACG launched an internal review of membership value in 2000. Under the direction of ACG member and research expert Laura Matz, ACG funded a six-month member survey. Using electronic survey tools and in-depth personal interviews with leaders and staff, the outcome was the first comprehensive snapshot of ACG value to the entire membership. The survey results were published in 2001, and ACG staff and board organized to systematically address areas needing review and improvement. Craig Stokely of The Stokely Partnership and member of the marketing committee led the strategic planning session that was informed by the Matz survey results.

The initial PR program with FRB achieved significant visibility for ACG in 1999 and 2000. National publications like *The Wall Street Journal, Business Week, Crain's Chicago Business, INC., CFO, Entrepreneur,* and many local papers carried ACG news. "Deal-a-Minute" was the headline of a front-page story of the *WSJ* that broke opening day of InterGrowth 1999 to great buzz and excitement. But the cost-benefit relationship with the firm lessened over time, and in July 2001, ACG terminated the relationship with FRB.

Less than a year later, ACG would sign a branding agreement with Landor Associates and undertake a two-year program that solidified a brand that had wobbled through the chapters in their use of name, logos, colors, and description. The branding program exceeded budget, but it is still widely held by members close to the program that its value outweighed cost overruns.

The branding program and its immediate outcomes of collateral material for InterGrowth, membership, and sponsorship, the acg.org overhaul, an eight-minute fiftieth-anniversary highlight CD distributed to all chapters in a rebranded, new-member notebook, gave ACG visual and verbal unity to showcase in the global financial marketplace it preferred.

Dealmakers Survey Expands Reach

The Dealmakers survey found a new partner in 2003 under the direction of Patrick Hurley, ACG vice president of marketing. Thomson Financial and ACG worked the first year with Magnet Communications, the PR firm involved with Landor in ACG's branding initiative, to deliver an electronic dealmaker's survey to nearly two thousand members and readers. The results were reported to major business media, which responded enthusiastically. For the first time, ACG leaders took media interviews about survey results. The initiative would add the Reuter's name in 2004—after the Thomson-Reuters merger—and the ACG-Thomson-Reuter's Dealmaker's Survey continues as a widely publicized semi-annual endeavor today, with dozens of media reporting the results. The media rollout has broadened to include CNBC, YouTube, *Wall Street Journal*, Dow Jones, and other major business press internationally.

ACG marketing materials after branding, mid 2000's

New Member Magazine Nets Broad Rewards

The ACG-Thomson-Reuters relationship did not stop with the survey. Again with Patrick Hurley's leadership, ACG negotiated with Thomson Financial to partner with ACG to make Thomson's business publication, *Mergers and Acquisition, the Dealmakers Journal (MAJ)*, an ACG member benefit. Several pages were dedicated to ACG news, folding in the *ACG Network* content, and the ACG logo was positioned on the cover. *ACG Network*, which had been published for ten years, ceased publication in January 2005. During the partnership formation, Thomson sold its publishing arm to Investcorp. under the name Sourcemedia, which continues to publish *MAJ* today.

Store Mini-Launch

At ACG InterGrowth in Colorado Springs (2001), ACG's marketing committee under ACG Denver member Bob Prangley expanded the discussion of making ACG labeled items available to chapters. In Colorado was opportunity to buy golf bags, jackets, hats, and more, and earn a profit for ACG. It took seven years for the online retail store to become a reality. ACG New York President and ACG Global Board Member Bobby Blumenfeld, who, like Mr. Prangley, had extensive prior retail experience, set up a committee to launch the ACG Online Retail Store. Working with acting ACG Global President Brad Hughes, staff member Dale West, and James Easterling, ACG legal counsel, the online store launched July 15, 2008. It served two purposes: it ensured brand consistency and it brought economies of scale for improved pricing to the chapters. The store closed in 2011. Chapter loyalties to local suppliers and a change in the national supplier's interest in ACG were key reasons for the final decision.

In the Televised News

In 2005, under Dan Varroney's leadership, ACG gained televised coverage in the financial media. CNBC, Fox News, NASDAQ's Opening Bell were among the programs that aired commentary from ACG staff and volunteers.

The broadcasts have continued into 2011 with Gary LaBranche, Den White, and others discussing ACG on CNBC, Fox, and more.

Highlights of ACG over the year, InterGrowth, ACG Capital Connection, and chapter events such as ACG Cleveland Deal Maker Awards are just some of the internally produced videos available on ACG's website and on ACG.TV in most recent years.

By 2011, ACG had developed efforts to reach audiences through various channels, including Twitter, Facebook, and via the Executive Insight Network, a project sponsored by SAP.

The Essential Network, launched in 2009 and shared by ACG Global and every chapter, now attracts nearly 1 million visits a year. The online member directory, ACG CapitalLink, and ACG JobSource are used thousands of times every week. The $500k investment in the Essential Network, under a project led by ACG Chicago CEO Craig Miller, has proven to be a vital part of the ACG member experience and an outreach to potential members.

CHAPTER 11

GOVERNANCE

GOVERNANCE FINE-TUNING
ACG CHAPTERS AND ACG "INTERNATIONAL"

ACG began in New York City. The association flourished there exclusively for several years. Eventually, because of the distance factor, ACG members formed additional chapters in Chicago, Toronto, and Los Angeles.

The four chapters decided to create an opportunity for all ACG members to come together and network. They established the first InterGrowth conference in 1972. They staged it in Mexico City to reflect the long-range international aspiration of the organization. Additionally, 1972 was the first year for a central body—called "international" for three decades and in the twenty-first century changed to "global"—to form the first board and elect its first president. He was Tom Smith of the Chicago office of Ernst & Ernst.

Struggle for Justification of Central Office Begins ...

Mr. Smith and his successors struggled to create value so that the chapters would pay for operations of a central office that was doing little more than running InterGrowth. InterGrowth was expensive and attended by only 10 percent of the membership for many years. To smooth the waters, the global leaders made personal visits to chapters that clamored the most, pitching that "the whole is better than the sum of its parts." For the most part, these leaders were successful in their cries for unity ... until the sands started shifting again.

... And Continues

At the start of the 1990s, the ACG Global board of directors was unwieldy, according to directors at the time. It was large and unfocused and faced a faltering organization in considerable debt. Now big and small chapters questioned the value of the central organization. Chapters like Boston, Los Angeles, and others showcased an array of programs that offered networking and knowledge. They had their own administrative staffs capable of handling meetings and dues administration. The same complaint was surfacing: the central office and InterGrowth did not offer enough value for the time and expense.

The board of ACG nonetheless held on to the belief that the whole is greater than the sum of its parts. It was motivated to add value that chapters would see, and it took action. It solved the debt problems and tapped one of its own members to lead a strategic planning session. The outgrowth gave new direction to the board and its new chief staff officer Carl Wangman.

First Public Relations Plan, Regional Meetings

InterGrowth management was only one of the "central office" assignments. Mr. Wangman's firm hired a professional PR firm that created new channels of communication with members through newsletters and data exchange. Iacuzzi Associates issued press releases, launched surveys, and advertised in industry publications.

Like his predecessors, Mr. Wangman and various officers of the board made personal visits to each chapter, but they also offered a new venue that took root in the form of Regional Leadership meetings. These smaller groupings of chapter leaders, held in the northern, southern, eastern, and western United States, would discuss best practices among themselves. These meetings grew into the chapter leadership best-practice exchange held first at InterGrowth at the end of the century.

The Wangman staff and volunteer leaders held membership growth and retention contests and removed roadblocks that had prevented members from transitioning from one chapter to another in the event of a professional relocation. The expansion of the member directory, the first significant sponsorships at InterGrowth, and the diversification of the InterGrowth program addressed issues the chapters raised. Positions of membership, marketing, corporate member affairs, international expansion, and online communications were created on the board of directors to give clear and new direction to the organization. Centralizing dues billing and filing legal documents were moves happily received by most chapters and their administrators.

By the mid-'90s, ACG chapters had quieted their protests and for the most part climbed on board, accepting the value of an ACG national headquarters.

New Leadership Pool Wanting More

While these internal improvements were happening, other rumblings in the marketplace challenged the organization to change and adapt again. The rise of the private equity firms in the middle market and the advent of the Internet for commercial use became sea changes for ACG. As the century drew to a close, these two entities would entrench themselves in ACG and test the chapter/headquarters relationship in new and significant ways.

Larger Meetings Net Big Profits

Private equity brought a hunger for change and an aggressive "let's-get-it-done-now" attitude; the Internet brought instant communication. The ACG board and staff rethought how to create value for chapters and members. Bigger chapters were taking giant steps of their own—creating successful meetings that rivaled InterGrowth. In Los Angeles, sponsorship money flowed, and celebrities took the podium. Boston, New York, Chicago, and Cleveland embraced the format of large meetings on home turf where financing and deals were showcased as never before. The birth of the ACG Capital Connection in Los Angeles and Boston opened the floodgates, and InterGrowth with its own ACG Capital Connections in 2003 brought the event to all the membership. ACG Capital Connections spread like wildfire.

Rebranding Lays Groundwork for Administrative Change

The first three years of the twenty-first century continued the expansion of membership and chapter events throughout North America and into Europe. The ACG brand—and its visual and verbal inconsistencies—was gaining notice. A brand-development program launched by the ACG Global board began in 2003. The volunteer committee with oversight for the brand-development process had broad representation from chapter leadership in North America and Europe and worked closely with the well-regarded firm leading the exercise, Landor Associates. The new ACG brand rollout in 2004 brought visual/verbal cohesion to ACG, but attaining it was costly. An attempt by the ACG Global board to gain chapter assistance to accommodate the budget shortfall caused by the branding process failed.

Full-Time President & CEO Heralds Governance Change

More representation throughout ACG

Meanwhile, ACG leaders organized around a vision of ACG staffing that expanded the leader's role to a CEO who had his own team devoted exclusively to ACG. In late 2004, the ACG Global board met in a strategic planning session led by consultant and author Ram Charan, who helped clarify the power of the organization and challenged the board to become more strategic in its thinking. An outcome of the strategic plan was a governance committee of the board whose work created a more representative board, one that ensured a balance of large and small geographically diverse chapters.

The contract with The Center for Association Growth ended in the first quarter of 2005, and Dan Varroney in June of that year assumed the president & CEO position, setting up ACG's first independent headquarters in Palatine, Illinois. Varroney left ACG in September 2007. Brad Hughes, ACG's CFO, assumed the duties of interim president and CEO.

On September 1, 2008, Gary LaBranche, CAE, FASAE, joined the ACG Global staff as president and CEO. ACG headquarters was soon moved to the city of Chicago in April 2009. A staff of fourteen professionals was soon recruited to manage daily operations and carry out the strategic plan adopted by the Global board. The ACG Global board of twenty-eight, including eleven chapter representatives, nine directors at large, six officers, and two InterGrowth chairs, retains its strategic focus, advised by a number of standing committees.

Over the years, the governing structure has shown the elasticity of an organization of impressive growth and development; it has also entrenched itself in a representative format to gain the best input from the most members.

As 2011 dawned, ACG global had annual revenue of $8 million and reserves of more than $2 million. ACG chapters collectively generate more than $16 million in revenue and have more than $11 million in reserves.

The Association for Corporate Growth is well funded and organized, with a growing membership and global footprint and is strongly positioned to achieve the mission of "driving middle-market growth" long into the future.

ACG Ringing the Bell at NASDAQ 2009

ACKNOWLEDGMENTS

We have many to thank for this project and the story we told. Alan Gelband and Bobby Blumenfeld inspired the idea of writing an ACG history, made contact with us, and offered that ACG New York pay for the project. We surmise that Ken Kovalcik was a guiding angel from New York. Lou Halstead helped steer the ship.

Other influences whose vast ACG experience gave credibility to our work were Chicagoans Tom Smith and Fred Roberton, whom we interviewed at length some eight years ago, long before they left us. We were fortunate to uncover many of our notes from those dazzling face-to-face meetings.

The current ACG staff could not have been more helpful. Gary LaBranche, Carol Jezierski, Leslie Whittet, John O'Loughlin, and Greg Fine provided a variety of information, leads, data, and direction. Carol opened the storage closet in Palatine to us as mice darted under foot. Jim Easterling opened his office and ACG legal archives; he answered several phone queries as well. Brad Hughes, recently retired from ACG Global, gave important insight into developments during the first decade following 2000.

We started with a listing of ACG presidents who became our lead interview candidates. We continued with interviews of leaders in the four chapters we covered: New York, Chicago, Toronto, and Los Angeles. We sent this list of some sixty people e-mails describing the project and asked for their input, either written or by phone. In many, many cases, phone conversations offered the quotations that give life and color to the record.

These conversations took no prodding on our part. To a number, the individuals, located in North America and Europe, gave their immediate time and attention to our questions, often offering more detail than what was asked. Initial interviews were often followed by e-mails and more phone calls to clarify or augment a point. All of it informed our thinking and writing.

We heard many times about the powerful mentoring system that exists from one leader to the next and the lifelong friendships formed en route. That phenomenon gave impetus to our title.

And we regret that many amusing anecdotes—like Hunt Whitacre's recollection of junk-bond king Mike Milken of Drexel speaking to the gathered ACG throng "with fire in his eyes"—will have to wait for volume two.

We've listed other generous contributors in alphabetical order and thank each of them for helping develop the first chapter that covers six decades.

Our deep gratitude to Dan Adamori, Burt Alimansky, Andrew Baird, Jim Blaising, Jim Bondoux, Michael Carr, Bob "Coach" Coffey, Barbara Corder, Charlie Downer, Harry Fendrich, Gary Fiebert, George Gingerelli, John Gullman, Diane Harris, Renate Herbst, Walt Howiler, Patrick Hurley, Dick Israel, Jay Jester, Paul Johnson, Rakesh Kaul, Bill Killian, Harald Klien, Joan McCarthy, Ed McGrath, Craig Miller, Chad Murrin, Phil Nielsen, Clifford Pearl, Pat Pickford, Bob Prangley, Donald Reed, Andy Rice, Russ Robb, Larry Roberts, Warren Rosenthal, Bill St. John, Steve Slavin, Harris Smith, George Stevenson, Craig Stokely, Dave Studeman, Jim Tucker, Connie Tuerk, Franz von Bradsky, Russ Warren, Hunt Whitacre, and Dennis White.

Peter Coffey, Jeri Harman, and Paul Stewart helped us with key transitional detail in the "executive suite" during this century. Their insight proved invaluable.

Many of our first sources alluded to secondary sources that are mentioned in the history—Patricia Buus, Debbie Victory, Joe Wingard, Dan Varroney, Jack Derby, Calvin Navatto, Richard Haskel, and many others—but were not interviewed independently. You'll find their names and titles when we could locate them and acknowledge their significance and influence on ACG.

There is much more to tell, so many others we didn't talk with. More than fifty chapters are not represented here, chapters that have driven and shaped ACG. Their sagas are yet to be written; their leaders and executives yet to be heard and quoted.

We thank many of you for giving us the opportunity to start the story.

—Judith and Carl

ABOUT THE AUTHORS

Carl A. Wangman has spent the better part of his professional career as an association executive. He has owned three different association-management companies. He served proudly as the chief staff officer for ACG from 1990 to 2005 during a period of rapid growth for the association. In 2006, he received the first ACG Lifetime Service Achievement Award. He also was honored by the Association Management Company Institute in 2011 with its Lifetime Achievement Award.

A history major with honors from Yale University, Carl maintains active interest in Yale by interviewing high school seniors who have applied for admission.

He lives in Glenview, Illinois, with his wife, Janice, who also served ACG. Their children, Brett and Marcie, are today the active principals in their association-management company. Blair, another son, is director KPMG Advisory with KPMG LLP in Chicago.

Carl Wangman, Chief Staff Officer ACG Global 1990-2005

Judith Q. Iacuzzi, ACG Marketing Director 1994-2005

Judith Q. Iacuzzi's interest in ACG stems to the mid-'90s, when she was engaged as the association's marketing and communications director, a position she held for eleven years. A trained journalist with a master's from Medill's School of Journalism at Northwestern, she has been touting the value of non-profit organizations and associations for thirty years. She worked closely with Carl Wangman on the delivery of service throughout The Center for Association Growth's management of ACG. She thoroughly enjoyed her work and the relationships that formed in the process.

Judy resides with her husband, Tony, in Evanston, Illinois. They have three grown children. This is her first history and one of many collaborative writing projects with Carl. She is currently writing a memoir.

ACG Global chairs

FIRST NAME	LAST NAME	COMPANY	CHAPTER	YEAR SERVED
Thomas	Smith	(Deceased)	Chicago	1972–1973
Peter	Hilton	(Deceased)	New York	1973–1974
Frederick	Roberton	(Deceased)	Chicago	1974–1975
Anthony	Hass	AgriCapital Corporation	New York	1975–1976
Donald	Reed	The Reed Group of Florida	Chicago	1976–1977
Harold	Fleming	(Deceased)	New York	1977–1978
Carl	Hagelin	(Deceased)	Los Angeles	1978–1979
Robert	Coffey	Geneva Merger & Acquisition Services of Canada Inc.	Toronto	1979–1980
Thomas	Chmielewski	(Deceased)	Houston	1980–1981
Stephen	Helpern	Helpern	Chicago	1981–1982
Gary	Fiebert	Gilbert Tweed Associates, Inc.	New York	1982–1983
Harry	Fendrich	CAM Interests, Inc.	Dallas	1983–1984
James	Dwyer	Dwyer & Associates	New York	1984 –1985
Walter	Howiler	Kirk Paper Company	Orange County	1985–1986
Gerald	Hoag	A. T. Kearney, Inc.	Dallas	1986–1987
Huntley	Whitacre	RJR Nabisco, Inc.	New York	1987–1988
James	Blaising	Higgins, Marcus & Lovett, Inc.	Los Angeles	1988–1989
Philip	Nielsen	A. C. Nielsen	Chicago	1989–1990
Kenneth	Kovalcik	(Deceased)	New Jersey	1990–1991
Ronald	Robison	Trust Company of the West	Los Angeles	1991–1992

FIRST NAME	LAST NAME	COMPANY	CHAPTER	YEAR SERVED
Alan	Gelband	Alan Gelband & Co, Inc.	New York	1992–1993
Edward	McGrath	Edward McGrath & Co	San Francisco	1993–1994
Russell	Warren	The TransAction Group, Inc.	Cleveland	1994–1995
William	Killian	Aqua-Chem, Inc.	Tampa Bay	1995–1996
Lawrence	Roberts	Rocket Ventures II, LLC	Portland	1996–1997
Diane	Harris	Hypotenuse Enterprises	New York	1997–1998
Charles	Conner	Bowles Hollowell Conner & Co.	Carolinas	1998–1999
Conrad	Tuerk	Tuerk & Associates	Orange County	1999–2000
Christopher	Gebelein	Private Equity Growth Advisors	Chicago	2000–2001
Russell	Robb	Atlantic Management Company	Boston	2001–2002
John	Gullman	USBX Advisory Services	South Florida	2002–2003
Charles	Downer	Downer & Company	Boston	2003–2004
James	Tucker	Spectral Dynamics, Inc.	Orange County	2004–2005
Peter	Coffey	Michael Best & Fredrich LLP	Wisconsin	2005–2006
Patrick	Hurley	MidMarket Capital	Philadelphia	2006–2007
Paul	Stewart	PS Capital Partners	Wisconsin	2007–2008
Harris	Smith	Grant Thornton	San Francisco	2008–2009
Den	White	McDermott, Will & Emery	Boston	2009–2010
Michael	Carr	BAC Investments	Los Angeles	2010–2011
Andy	Rice	The Jordan Company	Chicago	2011–2012

CHAPTER INCEPTION DATES

Inception Date	Chapters
2004	101 Corridor
2007	Arizona
1974	Atlanta
2004	Austria
1979	Boston
2005	Calgary
1996	Central Texas
1990	Charlotte
1968	Chicago
2009	China
1993	Cincinnati
1981	Cleveland
2005	Columbus
2001	Connecticut
2010	Czech Republic
1974	Dallas/Fort Worth
1998	Denver
1984	Detroit
2004	France
2006	Frankfurt
2005	Holland
1975	Houston
2004	Indiana
2002	Kansas City
2008	Kentucky

Inception Date	Chapters
1972	Los Angeles
2005	Louisiana
1983	Maryland
1966	Minnesota
1989	National Capital
2010	Nebraska
2003	New Jersey
1954	New York
1999	North Florida
1984	Orange County
2006	Orlando
1986	Philadelphia
1986	Pittsburgh
1997	Portland
1996	Raleigh Durham
2006	Rhein-Ruhr
1996	Richmond
1984	San Diego
1976	San Francisco
2001	Seattle
1985	Silicon Valley
1982	South Florida
2011	Spain
1985	St. Louis
1997	Tampa Bay
2004	Tennessee
1971	Toronto
1999	United Kingdom
2003	Utah
2004	Vancouver
1999	Western Michigan
1987	Wisconsin

INTERGROWTH 1972−2012

Date	Location	Hotel	Chair
1972	Mexico City	Camino Real	Frederick Roberton, Design Consultants
			Program John May
1973	Boca Raton, Florida	Boca Raton Hotel & Club	Harold Fleming, Dexter Corp.
		46 ladies in attendance	*Program Kermit Brandt IC Industries*

The Impact of Government Policies on Corporate Growth in the '70s

1974	Phoenix, Arizona	Arizona Biltmore Hotel	Carl Hagelin, Marshall & Stevens
			Program Wm. Van Buren Merck & Co.

Corporate Development for Results, Not Theory

1975	Bermuda	Southampton Princess	Robert Coffey, Ernst & Young
			Program, Nevil Thomas Nevco Invest.

Managing Growth in a Period of Uncertainty

1976	Hot Springs, Virginia	The Homestead	Kermit Brandt, IC Industries
			Program, Gary Fox Ernst & Ernst

Growth: More Free or Regulated

Date	Location	Hotel	Chair
1977	Miami, Florida	Doral Country Club & Hotel	Muryl Olinger, Arthur Young & Company
			Program, Earl Bolton, Booz Allen Acquisition Services

Balanced Growth

Date	Location	Hotel	Chair
1978	Phoenix, Arizona	Arizona Biltmore	Frank Della Corte, Hill & Knowlton
			Program, Jerry Wiens

The Evolving Pattern of Corporate Growth

Date	Location	Hotel	Chair
1979	Palm Beach	The Breakers	James Adams, Fry Consultants
			Program, Marcus White, VP Texon

Understanding Current Influences Affecting Corporate Growth

Date	Location	Hotel	Chair
1980	San Diego	Hotel del Coronado	Stephen Halpern, Halpern Inc.

Corporate Growth—Coping with a Changing Environment

Date	Location	Hotel	Chair
1981	Boca Raton, Florida	Boca Raton Hotel and Club	William Potter, Foreman & Dyess

Planning for Growth in an Era of Shortages

Date	Location	Hotel	Chair
1982	Scottsdale, Arizona	The Registry Resort	Kenneth Bodenstein, Duff & Phelps, Inc.

Corporate Growth in a Deregulated Environment

Date	Location	Hotel	Chair
1983	Palm Springs, California	Marriott Rancho Las Palmas	James Dwyer III, Dwyer & Assoc.

Creative Strategies for Corporate Growth

Date	Location	Hotel	Chair
1984	Phoenix, Arizona	Arizona Biltmore	Gerald Hoag, A. T. Kearney, Inc.

Growth Strategies in a Transition Economy

Date	Location	Hotel	Chair
1985	Boca Raton, Florida	Boca Raton Hotel & Club	Huntley Whitacre, RJR Nabisco, Inc.

In Search of Growth: Corporate Revitalization

Date	Location	Hotel	Chair
1986	Scottsdale, Arizona	The Registry	James Blaising, Higgins, Marcus & Lovett, Inc.

Growth Strategies in an International Setting

Date	Location	Hotel	Chair
1987	Naples, Florida	The Ritz-Carlton Hotel	Philip Nielsen, A.C. Nielsen Company

Successful Strategies in a Maturing Economy

Date	Location	Hotel	Chair
1988	Tucson, Arizona	The WestIn La Paloma	Mark H. Friedman, M. H. Friedman Company

Mergers and Acquisitions and Corporate Development Post-Reagan

Date	Location	Hotel	Chair
1989	Palm Beach, Florida	The Breakers	Ronald E. Robison, Trust Company of the West

Global Growth Strategies for the 1990s

Date	Location	Hotel	Chair
1990	Phoenix, Arizona	Arizona Biltmore	Donald V. Smith, Houlihan, Lokey, Howard & Zukin

Changing Issues and Strategies for the 1990s

Date	Location	Hotel	Chair
1991	Boca Raton, Florida	Boca Raton Hotel & Club	R. Edward McGrath, CAMA, Inc.

Creating Value …

Date	Location	Hotel	Chair
1992	Scottsdale, Arizona	Scottsdale Princess	Thomas J. Corrigan, G.E. Capital

Beyond 2000

Date	Location	Hotel	Chair
1993	Orlando, Florida	Hyatt Regency Grand Cypress	Patricia A. Buus, The Lethridge Group, Inc.

Doing More with Less: Corporate Growth Today

Date	Location	Hotel	Chair
1994	Scottsdale, Arizona	Scottsdale Princess	James A. Bondoux, The Fremont Group

Acquisitions and Divestitures: Delivering Corporate Growth and Renewal

Date	Location	Hotel	Chair
1995	Palm Beach, Florida	The Breakers	David P. Ruwart, Plunkett & Cooney

New Paradigms of Growth: Deals & Strategies to Maximize Growth and Shareholder Value

Date	Location	Hotel	Chair
1996	La Jolla, California	Sheraton Grande at Torrey Pines	Charles H. Conner, Jr., Bowles Hollowell Conner & Co.

Silver Anniversary 25 Years of InterGrowth

Date	Location	Hotel	Chair
1997	San Antonio, Texas	Hyatt Regency Hill Country	Franz von Bradsky, Green Tree Capital

Thinking Outside the Box

Date	Location	Hotel	Chair
1998	Ponte Vedra Beach, Fla.	Marriott at Sawgrass Resort	Conrad J. Tuerk, Tuerk & Assoc.

Sustaining Your Company's Growth

Date	Location	Hotel	Chair
1999	Palm Springs, California	Rancho Las Palmas Marriott Resort	Russell Robb, O'Conor Wright Wyman, Inc.

How to Do It

Date	Location	Hotel	Chair
2000	Tampa, Florida	Saddlebrook Resort	John Gullman, Corporate Finance Partners

Al Reid, Program Chair

Make It Happen

Date	Location	Hotel	Chair
2001	Colorado Springs, Colorado	The Broadmoor	K. Clark Childers, Offutt, Childers & Putnam, P.C.

Building Toward the Future

Date	Location	Hotel	Chair
2002	Orlando, Florida	Hyatt Regency Grand Cypress	Peter L. Coffey, Michael Best Fredrich LLP
	What's Next?		
2003	San Diego, California	Hotel del Coronado	John T. Whates, Deloitte & Touche LLP
	IG32: Seal the Deal		
2004	Boca Raton, Florida	Boca Raton Resort and Club	Ron Kerdasha, LaSalle Bank
2005	Palm Springs, California	JW Marriott Desert Springs Resort & Spa	Ardelle St.George, St.George & Carnegie
	Make the Connection!		
2006	Orlando, Florida	Hyatt Regency Grand Cypress	Bev Landstreet, Proudfoot Consulting
	The 35th Annual Conference		
2007	Phoenix, Arizona	Arizona Biltmore & Spa	Jeri Harman, Allied Capital
2008	Orlando, Florida	Marriott World Center Resort	Harris Smith, Grant Thornton
2009	Las Vegas, Nevada	Wynn Las Vegas	Thomas Walton, Joy Global Brands
2010	Miami, Florida	Fontainebleau Hotel	Stuart Johnson, Barns & Thornburg
2011	San Diego, California	Manchester Grand Hyatt	Jack Helms, Lazard Middle Market
	March On		
2012	Dallas, Texas	Gaylord Texas Hotel	Douglass Tatum, The Co-Investment Partnership

Jay Jester, Managing Director, Audax Group, leading
panel at ACG InterGrowth in 2004

Secretary of State James Baker at ACG InterGrowth in Boca Raton 2004

The Center for Association Growth Staff at ACG
InterGrowth in Palm Springs 2005

Newt Gingrich at ACG InterGrowth in Las Vegas 2009

Art Laffer (Reagan Economic Director and father of the Laffer
Curve) at ACG InterGrowth Miami Beach 2010

Michael Hayden (former Director CIA and NSA) at
ACG InterGrowth in Miami Beach 2010

Jim Collins (author) at ACG InterGrowth San Diego 2011

General Stanley McChrystal at ACG InterGrowth in San Diego 2011

Steven Forbes at ACG InterGrowth

ACG InterGrowth in Dallas 2012

Volunteer Awards

ACG Meritorious Service and ACG Lifetime Achievement Award

2010:
Meritorious Service Award:
Dan Amadori
Mark Jones
Jim Marra
Harris Smith
Stuart Gruskin (posthumously)
Lifetime Achievement Award: Charles Downer

2009:
Meritorious Service Award:
Ed Fisher
Richard Jaffe
Mark Kuehn
Paul Stewart

2008:
Meritorious Service Award:
Don Feldman
Lifetime Achievement Award: Alan Gelband

2007:
Meritorious Service Award:
Robert Blumenfeld
Nancy Halwig
Jack Derby

2006:
Meritorious Service Award:
Joe Chapman
Harald Klien
Craig Miller
Jim O'Donnell
Ardelle St.George
Lifetime Achievement Award: Carl Wangman

Jim Tucker, ACG Global Chairman 2004-2005, presents Meritorious
Service Award to Den White at ACG InterGrowth 2005

2005:
Meritorious Service Award:
Sid Jaffe
George Stevenson
Den White

2004:

Meritorious Service Award:

Ron Kerdasha

Robert Barker

John Gullman

Ben Proctor

Lee Koehn

2003:

Meritorious Service Award:

Bailey S. Barnard

Gary D. Gilson

Kenneth E. Jones

Peter L. Coffey

Joseph Inge

Gary I. Levenson

2002:

Meritorious Service Award:

Cordell Berge

Jeri J. Harman

Renate D. Herbst

Jay C. Jester

Robert N. Rubin

2001:

Meritorious Service Award:

Lawrence W. Roberts

James D. Tucker

2000:

Meritorious Service Award:

Peter Blazier

Mark Borkowski

T. Patrick Hurley

Conrad J. Tuerk

1999:
Meritorious Service Award:
John F. Burns
Robert R. Prangley
Warner A. Rosenthal
Walter N. Sigall
Joseph A. Wingard

1998:
Meritorious Service Award:
Alan G. Johnson
Kenneth F. Kames
Howard M. Feldenkris

1997:
Meritorious Service Award:
Walter E. Howiler
Ronald A. Johnson
K. Clark Childers

1996:
Meritorious Service Award:
Philo Holcomb III
Bruce A. Johnson
William Luke, Jr.
David P. Ruwart (deceased)

1995:
Meritorious Service Award:
Alan Gelband
Diane Harris
Russell Robb
Deborah Victory
Carl A. Wangman

1994:
Meritorious Service Award:
Thomas J. Mahoney
Franz von Bradsky

1993:
Meritorious Service Award:
Paul O. Gaddis
Paul H. Johnson
William P. Killian
James Mahoney (posthumously)

1992:
Meritorious Service Award:
Charles H. Conner, Jr.
Robert P. Frisch
Janice Greenwald
Philip R. Nielsen
Thomas J. Smith

Epilogue

Join the conversation…

While putting together this book was a monumental task and we thank Carl Wangman and Judy Iacuzzi for the tremendous time, energy and passion they put into writing the first compilation of the history of ACG …with 57 chapters and close to 60 years of history, it was impossible to include every chapter and the great stories and experiences shared by members.

We invite you to add your voice to what we consider to be a living document that will continue to expand in the future. Please share your story and remembrance of past events by going to the website below and recording your information as well as photos.

ADD YOUR HISTORY AT www.acghistory.org

Alan Gelband, Gelband and Company
Bobby Blumenfeld, ACG New York, Executive Director

INDEX

A

Alimansky, Burt 28, 78, 162
Amadori, Dan 106, 110, 179

B

Baird, Andrew 162
Blaising, James 171
Blumenfeld, Bobby ix, 68, 72, 80–82, 86, 152, 161, 165
Bondoux, James 33, 162

C

Carr, Michael 120, 139, 162
Coffey, Peter 56, 162
Coffey, Robert 4, 102, 169
Corder, Barbara 104, 162

D

Downer, Chas 34, 42, 52, 60, 105, 162
Doyal, G. Thomas 40, 51, 137

E

Easterling, James 152

F

Fendrich, Harry 15, 131, 162
Fiebert, Gary 14, 77, 130, 162

G

Gelband, Alan ix, 22, 25, 28, 78, 161, 165, 166, 180, 183
Gingerelli, George 40, 43, 46, 149, 162
Gullman, John 50, 136, 162, 172, 181

H

Halstead, Lou 80, 86, 161
Harman, Jeri 56, 62, 117, 138, 162, 173
Harris, Diane 35, 37, 38, 40, 46, 162, 183
Herbst, Renate 52, 105, 162
Howiler, Walt 130, 162
Hughes, Brad 54, 152, 159, 161
Hurley, Patrick 51, 60, 63, 70, 71, 138, 139, 151, 152, 162, 182

I

Iacuzzi, Judith iii
Israel, Richard 114, 162

J

Jester, Jay 44, 57, 81, 106, 137, 162, 175
Jezierski, Carol 161
Johnson, Phil 5, 114, 115, 131, 162

K

Kaul, Rakesh 22, 26, 162
Killian, William 37, 38, 162
Klien, Harald 41, 94, 140, 141, 162, 180

L

Labranche, Gary 64, 65, 72, 140, 142, 153, 159, 161

M

Mccarthy, Joan 35, 141, 162
McgrAth, Ed 29, 162
Miller, Craig 68, 72, 95, 153, 162, 180
Mommsen, Jay 18
Murrin, Chad 162

N

Nielsen, Philip 171

O

O'loughlin, John 161

P

Pearl, Cliff 55, 162
Pickford, Pat 35, 39, 162
Prangley, Bob 137, 152, 162
Procter, Ben 57

R

Reed, Don 3, 76, 91
Rice, Andy 18, 24, 25, 93, 140, 162
Robb, Russ 28, 93, 135, 162
Roberts, Larry 37, 38, 162
Rosenthal, Warner 3, 13, 91

S

Slavin, Steve 92, 162
Smith, Harris 68, 69, 70, 162, 173, 179
Stevenson, George 92, 162, 181
Stewart, Paul 51, 52, 62, 63, 162, 180
St John, Wm 14, 15, 162
Stokely, Craig 51, 93, 150, 162
Studeman, Dave 52, 59, 60, 162

T

Tucker, James 4, 59, 66, 92, 162, 181
Tuerk, Connie 45, 162

V

Von Bradsky, Franz 39, 116, 162, 172,
183

W

Wangman, Carl iii, 18, 23, 28, 38, 40,
45, 60, 105, 129, 136, 137, 157,
164, 181, 185
Warren, Russ 34, 46, 162
Whitacre, Huntley 171
White, Den 70, 138, 153, 181
Whittet, Leslie 30, 51, 68, 141, 161
Wingard, Joe 117, 162